STREET STEEL

Also by Michael D. Janich:

Advanced Fighting Folders (video)
Blowguns: The Breath of Death
Breath of Death: The Blowgun Video (video)
Bullseyes Don't Shoot Back: The Complete Textbook of Point Shooting
   (with Col. Rex Applegate)
Fighting Folders (video)
Homemade Martial Arts Training Equipment
Knife Fighting: A Practical Course
Making It Stick: How to Throw Edged and Improvised Weapons
   for Sport and Self-Defense (video)
Martial Marksmanship: A Fighter's Guide to Close-Quarters Handgunning
   (video; with Andy Stanford)
Mastering Fighting Folders (VHS and DVD)
Mastering the Balisong Knife (VHS and DVD)
Mook Jong Construction Manual
Silat Concepts Form and Function (with Joseph Simonet)
Speak Like a Native: Professional Secrets for Mastering Foreign Languages
Switchblade: The Ace of Blades (with Ragnar Benson)

Street Steel: Choosing and Carrying Self-Defense Knives
by Michael D. Janich

Copyright © 1996 by Michael D. Janich

ISBN 10: 0-87364-886-2
ISBN 13: 978-087364-886-8

Printed in the United States of America

Published by Paladin Press, a division of
Paladin Enterprises, Inc.,
Gunbarrel Tech Center
7077 Winchester Circle
Boulder, Colorado 80301 USA
+1.303.443.7250

Direct inquiries and/or orders to the above address.

PALADIN, PALADIN PRESS, and the "horse head" design
are trademarks belonging to Paladin Enterprises and
registered in United States Patent and Trademark Office.

All rights reserved. Except for use in a review, no
portion of this book may be reproduced in any form
without the express written permission of the publisher.

Neither the author nor the publisher assumes
any responsibility for the use or misuse of
information contained in this book.

Visit our Web site at www.paladin-press.com

Front cover photos provided by James S. Piorek and Bud Nealy.
Additional photography by Sally Janich.

Street Steel

Choosing & Carrying Self-Defense Knives

Michael D. Janich

Paladin Press · Boulder, Colorado

Contents

I	Introduction	1
1	Basic Considerations in Choosing a Street Knife	3
2	Fixed Blade vs. Folding Knives	13
3	Carry Options for Fixed Blade Knives	19
4	Opening Folding Knives One-Handed	55
5	Carry Options for Folding Knives	75
	Conclusion	101

Warning

It is the reader's sole responsibility to research and comply with all local, state, and federal laws and regulations pertaining to the possession, carry and use of edged weapons. The author, publisher, and distributors of this book disclaim any liability from any damage or injuries that a reader of this book may suffer, as well as any damage or injuries to third parties from the reader of this book. The author, publisher, and distributors are not responsible for the use or misuse of the information contained herein. This book is presented *for information purposes only.*

Introduction

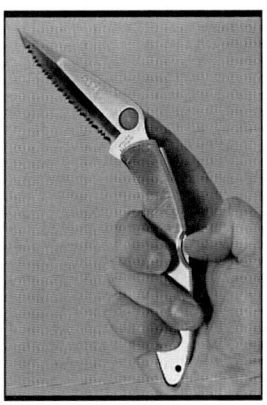

In recent years, most Americans have come to the realization that they are no longer safe from violent crime. Every day newspapers and television broadcasts are filled with stories detailing the barbaric crimes being committed against people from all walks of life and all levels of society. At the same time, in a misguided attempt to control the spread of violent crime, our elected officials are making every effort to restrict the sale of firearms or ban them altogether.

Average citizens, confronted with the fact that they are primarily responsible for defending themselves and yet are being denied the most effective means of doing so, are seeking defensive alternatives in greater numbers than ever before. Some enroll in self-defense classes, where they learn that unarmed combat skills, while useful, are a poor match for an armed attacker. Others purchase pepper sprays or other nonlethal weapons and desperately try to convince themselves that they are prepared in case they are attacked. Those who can purchase firearms do, only to find that, in most cases, they cannot legally carry them when they need them most.

So what is the answer? For many, the ideal weapon of compromise is the knife. Readily available, easily carried, and capable of delivering anything from a deterrent scratch to a lethal stab, the knife is once again gaining prominence as a defensive tool.

The public's quest for information on knife fighting has increased dramatically in recent years, and martial arts that focus on the use of the knife have gone from relative obscurity to immense popularity. There are now entire magazines, as well as numerous books and videos, devoted exclusively to the subject of knife fighting.

Knife manufacturers have also responded to the call by changing their focus to include a vast array of production knives in designs that are unmistakably intended for defensive applications.

Despite the vast amount of material now available on the defensive use of the knife and the large selection of knives on the market, no substantial information has been offered on how to actually choose a self-defense knife and carry it on a day-to-day basis. The art and technology of carrying concealed firearms is highly developed and frequently discussed in print; however, when it comes to carrying knives, there is precious little information available.

The objective of this book is to remedy this situation. In the chapters herein, you will find the information you need to select a self-defense knife that possesses all the design characteristics necessary to make it an effective street weapon. More importantly, however, you will learn how to choose and carry a knife that conforms perfectly to your style of dress, image, and habits.

The best fighting knife in the world won't do you a damned bit of good if it's sitting at home when you're attacked. Only when you are perfectly comfortable carrying a weapon will you carry it consistently. Learn how to make the right choice the first time so you can be sure your knife will be there when you need it most.

CHAPTER 1

Basic Considerations in Choosing a Street Knife

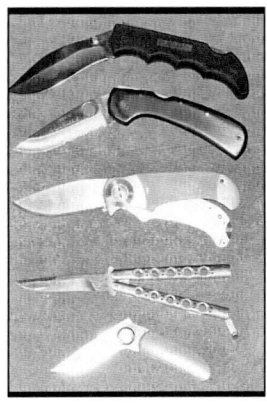

There are a number of basic criteria that you must remember when choosing a knife for self-defense. While the first rule of knife fighting is, of course, *have a knife*, not every knife is well suited to use as a defensive weapon.

The four basic considerations for a self-defense knife are blade length, blade shape, strength, and deployability. I consider all these factors equally important to a good defensive blade, so their presentation here is not in any order of importance.

The length of the blade you choose is important because it determines which targets you can hit successfully, as well as the ease with which a particular knife can be carried. A folding knife with a 2-inch blade is more than sufficient to cut the arteries in your opponent's wrist, but it is useless if you plan to stab him in the heart. Conversely, long blades like bowies and full-sized daggers are certainly capable of hitting any target you might choose; however, they are generally too large for everyday street wear. As a practical compromise between effectiveness and convenience, a blade length of 3 to 5 inches is recommended.

There are literally hundreds of blade shapes and styles available, based on hundreds of years of designing knives for different uses. In a fight, you're going to be doing one of two things: cutting or thrusting. Hence the basic requirements for a blade design are an edge that will cut effectively and a point that is sharp enough to penetrate, yet stout enough not to break if you miss a soft target and happen to hit a belt buckle, bone, or other resilient material. These may seem like pretty simple guidelines, but amazingly there are some very popular knives marketed as self-defense weapons that don't satisfy these requirements.

Like the point of your knife, the overall structure of your knife must also be strong enough to stand up to the abuse of a knife fight. For straight knives, a stout design with a substantial tang (the part of the blade that extends into the handle) is necessary. For folding knives, a strong, reliable locking mechanism is an absolute must. Anything less will probably cost you a few fingers (at the very least) the first time you try to stick your knife into somebody.

The final basic requirement of a self-defense knife is what I call deployability. Odds are you won't receive an engraved invitation to a knife fight. It will happen suddenly, without warning, and often while you are in a disadvantaged position. Deployability means the ability to get your knife from its carry position into the fully deployed, ready-to-cut-and-thrust mode quickly and from practically any position. Ideally, it also means being able to do this one-handed with either hand.

Deployability is obviously a function of both knife design and sheath style, so both must be taken into consideration when you make your choice. It is not uncommon to find a suitable straight blade fighting knife that is housed in a poorly designed and entirely inadequate sheath. (NOTE: If this happens, buy the knife anyway and have a suitable sheath made for it.) As far as straight knife design goes, the primary prerequisite for deployability are that its handle be large enough and suitably textured and shaped to provide a secure grip. The shape of the handle should also allow you to orient the knife in your hand immediately, using tactile sense alone. In other words, as soon as you get the knife in your hand you should know which way the primary edge and false edge (secondary cutting edge) are facing by touch alone. Additionally, the guard of the knife, if any, must not be excessively large or shaped so that it might snag on your own clothing when drawn from concealment.

Sheath design and placement are the other determining factors in the deployability of a fixed blade knife. We'll examine these issues in detail in later chapters.

Deploying folding knives is a slightly

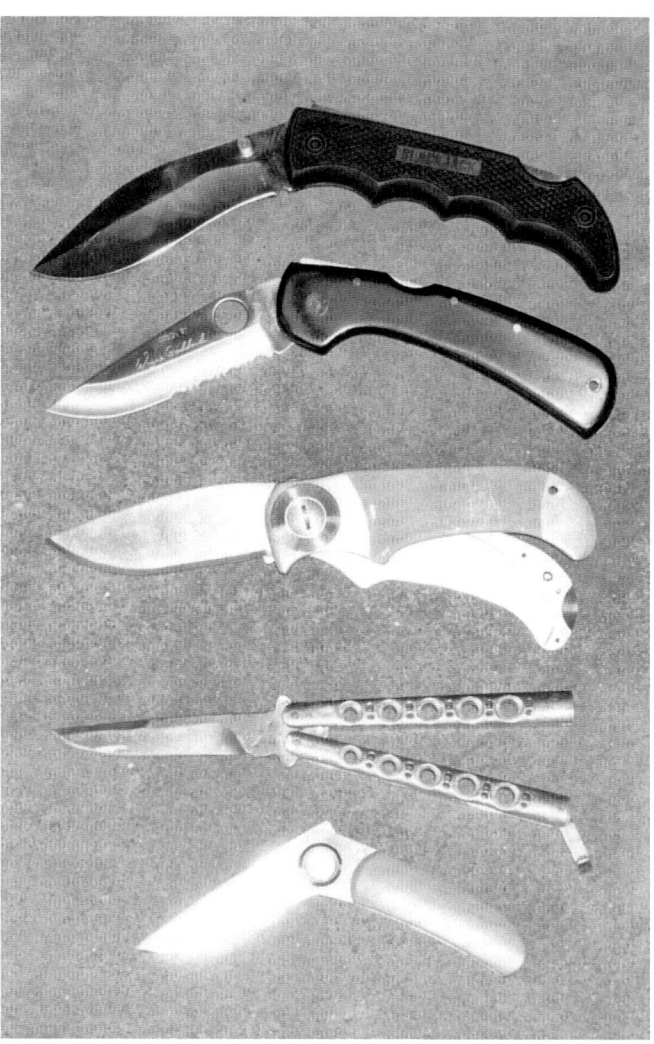

Strength is a primary concern when choosing a personal defense knife. This is particularly true for folding knives, which must have a strong and reliable locking mechanism to withstand the rigors of a knife fight.

A sampling of fixed blade knives suitable for personal protection. At the top (from left to right) are the Gryphon M10, a Gerber MK1 with a blued blade, and a Gerber Guardian. Beneath this is Bud Nealy's Aikuchi with damascus steel blade and neoprene handles and two boot knives made by the author.

different problem since two separate movements are required to bring them into action. In addition to being able to retrieve the knife quickly from its carry position, it is critical that you be able to open it quickly and with only one hand. Knives that require two hands or complicated movements to open are apt to be fumbled or dropped when brought into action under pressure. Unlike sword duels in movies, an opponent on the street is not likely to let you pick up a dropped blade so you can continue the contest on equal terms.

Although we'll get into the tactics of deploying personal defense knives later in this book, it is important to understand that pulling a knife is not an instantaneous response to an attack like the quick draw of a Western gunslinger or the *iai* (drawing and cutting in one stroke) of a Samurai. Ideally, by maintaining a high state of awareness, you'll be able to see an attack coming and either avoid it or have your knife in hand before things get serious. If you are truly surprised by an attack, your first move probably should not be to draw your weapon. You should concentrate on an initial defensive response, either unarmed or using whatever improvised weapons are at hand, so you can buy time and distance to draw your blade. Avoid adopting the mind-set that since you carry a knife it is your only means of defense. A knife, like any weapon, should complement your natural body weapons, not replace them.

The minimum criteria for a defense knife are just that: the absolute minimum qualities a knife must possess to be suitable for use as a weapon. Obviously, many knives satisfy these criteria, so how do you narrow down your choice? The answer is in your closet. *The primary determining factor in the selection of a self-defense knife is the way you dress.* The clothing you wear and the image you choose to project, more than anything else, determine what kind of knife you can carry.

As I mentioned earlier, the first rule of knife fighting is to have a knife. The whole purpose of a self-defense knife is having it with you when you need it. Too many people look only at a knife's potential as a weapon and choose knives which, though practical for carry on a belt or military load-bearing equipment, cannot be effectively carried and concealed in normal street dress. Knives that are too much hassle to carry will often be left at home or in a vehicle and will not be available when you need them.

A case in point . . . a number of years ago, I had a friend whose girlfriend was raped. With a little help, and without the encumbrance of the legal system, he personally ensured that justice was swiftly served and that the perpetrators were duly punished. Several months later, when these miscreants were again able to walk and eat solid food, they came after him. My friend decided that a knife was to be his defensive weapon of choice and

Knife drawing is not like the quick draw of the Old West. When attacked, your first action should not be to draw your knife but to defend yourself by any means possible. Here an unarmed defense is used to buy time to draw a knife. A downward stab is first parried and countered with an eye jab. With the attack temporarily negated and the attacker stunned, the knife can be drawn and brought into play.

BASIC CONSIDERATIONS IN CHOOSING A STREET KNIFE

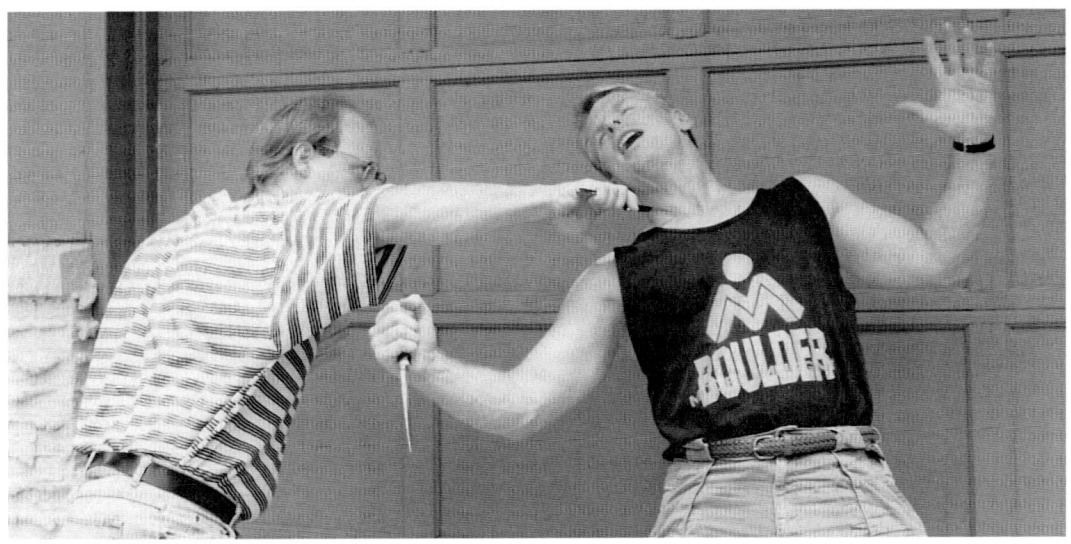

came to me for advice. I recommended a medium-sized folding knife equipped with a quick-opening blade attachment, much like the knife I carried at the time. He ignored my advice, bought a full-sized combat knife, and asked me to make a shoulder harness to carry it. I made the harness, which he wore comfortably for several weeks until the weather became too warm for the heavy jacket required to conceal the rig. He then purchased a large folding knife, which had tremendous potential as a weapon but was extremely heavy. It quickly became obvious to him that this knife couldn't be carried comfortably in his pocket and required a belt pouch. However, when he switched to the belt pouch carry, he found that he suddenly attracted lots of the wrong kind of attention from the campus police. Finally, he purchased the exact same model of knife I carried. He's now carried that knife daily for more than 10 years and wouldn't give it up for anything.

The first step in choosing a carry knife is to walk over to your closet and take a good look at the clothes you wear. Look at *everything* you wear and pay particular attention to your dress styles during different seasons. Look closely at the similarities and differences between your work clothes and your formal clothes and note any special clothing you might wear like running shorts or sweat pants. *Do not* disregard items of clothing that you only wear infrequently. If you're an average person, you will only be attacked infrequently and almost certainly without warning. Your goal must be to find a carry knife that is compatible with *all* your clothing styles so you can ensure that you are armed *all* the time.

You may be tempted to buy several different knives to carry in different positions, depending upon the style of dress you choose. For example, you might want to carry a folder in a belt sheath most of the time but switch to a boot knife carried in a shoulder harness during the winter months when you regularly wear a jacket. The problem with this approach is that, like all weapon handling skills, drawing a defensive knife must be a conditioned reflex. When you are confronted by a situation which demands that you respond by drawing and possibly using a weapon, your actions must be swift and automatic. If you normally carry your knife in a belt pouch and suddenly switch to another carry, when forced to respond to a situation, you will most likely fall back on conditioned reflex and reach for your belt pouch. By the time you realize that your knife isn't there, you will have lost valuable seconds and will have warned your attacker that you are armed with some kind of weapon (even if you can't seem to find it). If he has any sense, he won't wait for you to make another attempt to retrieve your weapon and will drop you immediately.

Closely related to your style of dress is your stature. Your height and physical body size figure strongly in determining the type of clothes you wear. They are also critically important to determining what type of weapons you can comfortably carry. A guy who is 6-foot-3 could conceivably carry a full-sized combat knife in a shoulder harness or inside-the-pants sheath and never know it was there. Someone who's five-foot-eight would have a much tougher time with such carries because of his smaller stature. He might be more at home with a clip-style folder carried in the front of his waistband. This carry style, on the other hand, might not work for a guy with a substantial beer belly who would have to dig around under his paunch every time he wanted to retrieve his knife.

In addition to making sure that your knife and carry system are compatible with your stature and all your styles of dress, you should also consider if they fit with the image you want to project. If you choose to carry a folder openly in a belt pouch, you are announcing to the world that you are armed with a knife. If you live on a ranch or work in a blue collar job, carrying a knife in that way would not attract undue attention.

Basic Considerations in Choosing a Street Knife

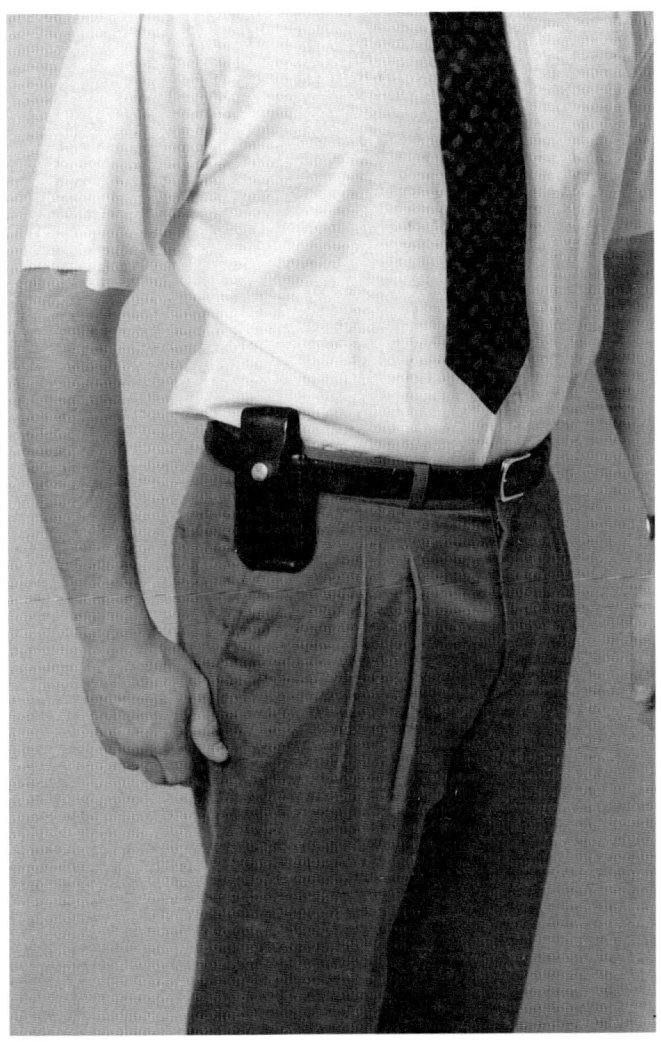

The image you want or need to maintain is also an important factor in your choice of knife carry. A belt pouch carry is fine for a blue collar worker, but might look out of place with a suit and tie.

Conversely, if you wear a coat and tie and work in an office environment where being openly armed would elicit a negative reaction, you'd be better off looking for another carry style. Think carefully about how others see you and the image you want or need to maintain in your everyday life before you choose a carry style. Remember that your carry style should not change when you take off your coat and tie and put on jeans and a T-shirt.

Another important factor in choosing a carry knife is the nature of your everyday activities. That new boot knife may feel great tucked away at the back of your waistband and you may be lighting fast drawing it with either hand. However, if you spend most of your work day seated in a vehicle, such an arrangement is not practical. Drawing a knife from the back of your waistband while in a vehicle and wearing a seat belt is frustration that need not be experienced to be understood. In such a situation, carrying the knife in the front of your waistband, in a shoulder harness, or even in your boot would be a better solution.

While on the subject of everyday activities, you need to consider whether you plan to make your blade serve double duty as a weapon and a utility tool. Knives are useful for cutting hundreds of other things besides flesh and are a good addition to everyone's personal equipment. Choosing a knife that can serve as both a tool and a weapon has two other important advantages. First, its utility function gives you a legitimate reason for carrying it and could significantly ease any legal or image hassles you may encounter if questioned by the authorities. Secondly, by using your knife consistently for everyday cutting jobs, you are constantly developing and refining your drawing and knife handling abilities. The skill you develop in this daily practice will obviously serve you well when it comes time to draw your knife under pressure.

One bit of advice—unless you live in a rural environment where a straight blade knife is socially accepted, stick with folding knives for combined utility/weapon use. Straight blades generally tend to make people, including cops and judges, very nervous. Whipping out a boot knife to cut the string on a package will probably shock most people and doesn't really support its function as a utility tool. If you choose to carry a pure fighting design for defense but need a utility knife as well, get a Swiss Army knife or similar pocketknife for everyday cutting. Such

Defensive knives that do double duty as utility tools can be more easily justified if found by the authorities or seen by others. The act of drawing and using your knife for everyday chores also helps hone your knife deployment skills.

A selection of folding knives suitable for personal defense use. They include (top row, left to right) a Wayne Goddard custom Clipit from Spyderco, the Spyderco Police Model, the Blackjack Folding Kukri, the Blackjack Mamba, (bottom row) the Wyoming Knife Company Powder River Folder, a Benchmade custom balisong, a Benchmade production balisong, and a Gerber Paul knife.

knives are so different from defensive blades that it is very unlikely you'll accidentally reach for it instead of your fighting knife. Keep your fighting knife tucked away out of sight until you need it and conduct regular, but private, practice sessions to master drawing it under pressure.

Obviously, if you ever use your knife to defend yourself or are searched by the police, there is likely to be some legal consequence. Laws regulating weapons are often poorly written, but knife laws are notoriously imprecise and ambiguous. The determination of what constitutes a legal or illegal knife or a legally or illegally carried knife is often up to the whim of the police and the courts. As such, the question of legality as it applies to carrying a knife for self-defense basically boils down to how much hassle you are willing to endure if your blade is found on your person. If you have to use your knife in a fight, you will do so because you fear for your own life or the life of a loved one. In that context, the legality of carrying that knife will be of secondary concern to simply ensuring your own survival. In such a case, the old saying "I'd rather be tried by twelve than carried by six" still rings true.

It is nevertheless a good idea to research the laws regarding the carrying of knives in your area and try to choose a knife that complies as closely as possible to the spirit of these laws. The best way to do this is to go to the local library and check the revised statutes for your state. If you live in or near a large city, also check any applicable municipal laws on the subject. Use the index to find the laws that pertain to weapons and make a photocopy of that section to retain for your reference. Make sure you get the most recent version, as laws can change frequently.

Odds are that the statute will prohibit weapons such as "dirks and daggers." Most laws use these terms but never offer precise definitions since they have both been applied to a variety of different knife designs throughout history. If you're lucky, the law might specify the legal blade length or specifically prohibit double-edged knives, giving you some guideline for what constitutes a legal carry knife. Otherwise, most knife laws can be interpreted so that *any* knife can be technically considered illegal.

What does all this really mean? Essentially, it means that the decision as to what constitutes an illegal knife (or an illegally carried knife) is entirely up to the police and the courts. In most cases, their determination is not based on any particular physical or design characteristics of the knife but rather the attitude and behavior of the person carrying it. In fact, it is quite possible that if your knife is found by the police and you exhibit a good attitude with the proper degree of feigned repent, you'll lose nothing more than your knife and a few minutes of your time. I've been carrying a knife every day for more than 20 years, many times in environments where they were strictly prohibited. To date, I have only had one confiscated and have suffered no legal hassles whatsoever.

The bottom line is that if you choose to carry a knife, try to make it comply as closely as possible to the guidelines specified in the laws in your area. If the laws are so ambiguous or your need for a substantial defensive blade is so acute that this can't be done, at least be aware of the legal risk you're taking and have the name of a good lawyer handy just in case. By the way, in case you hadn't guessed or failed to read the first few pages of this book, neither the author nor the publisher endorses the illegal carry of any type of weapon. Likewise, neither the author nor the publisher accepts any legal responsibility for actions taken by those who read this book.

One final note on legal issues: Although many knife writers suggest checking with your local police to find out what types of knives can be legally carried, I don't recommend it. I've tried it several times and have never gotten an answer that even came close to what the law actually described. Law enforcement officers are understandably afraid of facing knives on the street and aren't above telling a few white lies to discourage you from carrying a blade. They also know from actual experience that knife laws are so imprecise that it's impossible for them to say what type of knife would be ruled legal in court.

If, despite my advice, you do choose to query your local police about the legality of a particular knife, bring the knife in a sealed box and open the box in front of the officer. Better yet, bring a photo of the knife along with its dimensions. Walking up to the desk sergeant in a police station and pulling a knife out of your pocket can produce some interestingly unpleasant responses.

> **Knife Carry Checklist**
> - Is your knife design physically adequate for personal defense (with regard to blade length, blade shape, and strength)?
> - Is the carry option compatible with all of your dress styles?
> - Is the carry option consistent with the image you want to present?
> - Is the knife comfortable to carry in that position?
> - Is the knife easily retrieved one-handed with either hand?
> - Is the knife accessible when you are seated? In a vehicle? In a disadvantaged position?
> - If you carry your knife for both utility and personal defense, does it meet *both* needs adequately?
> - Are the legal consequences of carrying your knife more serious than you are willing to endure if it is found on your person?
> - Does the knife work effectively with your personal knife fighting style?

The final consideration in selecting your personal defense knife is your style of knife fighting. Take a critical look at the way you apply your knife in a fight and note the design characteristics required to make your techniques effective. For example, if you are partial to striking with the butt of the knife handle in addition to cutting and thrusting with the blade, you might want a knife with a long handle and a tapered pommel to facilitate such strikes and maximize their effect. Remember, though, that all the considerations outlined above still apply and are just as important to the knife's potential as a weapon.

By following these guidelines, you can choose a knife that will serve you well in a fight and, more importantly, can be carried comfortably enough so it will be there when you need it most.

Chapter 2

Fixed Blade vs. Folding Knives

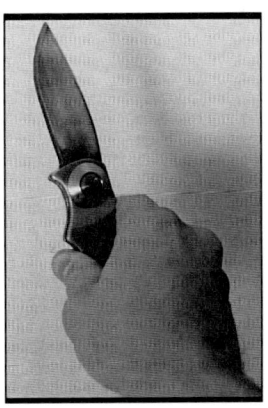

One of the first decisions you must make when shopping for a personal defense knife is whether to get a fixed blade (also called a straight blade or sheath knife) or a folding knife. A fixed blade knife is a knife that has its handle rigidly affixed to the blade. The handle is actually affixed to a portion of the blade called the tang, which extends into and sometimes completely through it. If the tang has the same profile as the handle and can be seen between the handle scales, the knife is a *full tang* design. If the handle completely surrounds the tang and the tang extends all the way to the butt of the knife, the knife is a *concealed tang* or *narrow tang* design. If the tang extends only partially through the handle, it is a *partial tang* knife.

Fixed blade knives offer several advantages over folding knives when it comes to self-defense applications. The first is strength. Since the blade and tang are one piece of contiguous steel, the knife is much stronger than any folding knife design. As mentioned earlier, strength is a highly desirable quality in a knife that may be called upon to penetrate through a leather jacket and continue through several inches of flesh. The worst failure typically experienced with a fixed blade knife is the point of the blade breaking off when thrust into a resilient target. Although this is not a good thing to have happen in the midst of a fight, it probably won't cause any immediate damage to you. Folding knife failures, on the contrary, cause such knives to live up to their name. On hard impact they could fold right onto the hand and fingers holding them.

Another advantage of fixed-blade knives is speed of deployment. Normally these knives will be carried in a sheath that is secured somewhere on the body. To draw the knife, the user simply grabs the handle and removes the knife from the sheath. He or she is now ready to go to battle. In some cases, knives will be retained in their sheaths by some type of strap or snap fixture that must be released to remove them. These are usually well designed for quick release and do little to slow down the process of drawing the knife. Folding knives, however, require two actions to bring them out into the open position: first the entire knife must be removed from its carry position, then the blade must be opened. The extra movements involved in drawing a folding knife and the enhanced possibility of fumbling the knife during the performance of these movements are distinct disadvantages that give the edge (forgive the pun) to fixed knives where speed is concerned. Folding knives are also nearly impossible to open quickly while wearing gloves.

The final advantage of a fixed blade is that it allows the use of a double-edged blade without posing any danger to the user. A double cutting edge is a distinct advantage on a fighting knife, since it makes penetration during thrusts much easier and more direct. It also allows the user to cut when withdrawing the knife straight back, eliminating the need to turn the knife edge into the target before pulling back. With rare exceptions, such as the excellent Applegate-Fairbairn Folding Knife, folding knives must be single edged. The reason is that the typical folder design requires that the back of the blade be exposed when the knife is closed. A sharpened back edge on a folder could cause a nasty cut when the user tries to retrieve it, especially if he's in a hurry. A second cutting edge on a sheath knife poses no danger to the user since it, too, is protected by the sheath.

Despite the advantages described above, fixed blades have their downside as well. For starters, they are not as convenient to carry as folding knives. As we've already established, knives that cannot be carried comfortably and conveniently are apt not to be carried at all. A fixed blade normally requires a sheath that is worn securely somewhere on the body so when the knife is drawn, the sheath stays in place. Strapping an 8-inch or longer piece of metal anywhere on your body will probably result in its jabbing, poking, or chafing you at some point during your daily activities.

Fixed blade knives also attract a lot of attention. In most areas of the United States, the carry of knives in general is not as socially accepted as it was 30 or 40 years ago. The idea that every well-prepared man or boy carries a pocketknife is no longer popular. As such, the carry of a fixed blade is considered much like carrying a gun. And, let's face it, the popular belief today is that the only people who carry weapons are cops and criminals. Law-abiding citizens are supposed to protect themselves from crime by moving to a better neighborhood, buying security systems for their home and car, and practicing dialing 911 a lot.

The image problem of a fixed blade knife need not be a problem, however, since the only people who should ever see it are hapless attackers into whom you will be trying to stick it. If you opt to carry a fixed blade for self-defense, practice drawing it at home or in private until the movements are second nature. When you carry it, keep it concealed all the time. If you need a knife for utility use, get a small pocketknife that won't raise any eyebrows and won't confuse you when the red flag goes up and it's time to reach for a weapon.

Folding knives which have blades that lock open rigidly make excellent personal defense knives and outshine fixed blades in two very important ways. First, they are extremely convenient to carry. Smaller knives can be carried unobtrusively in a pocket, and larger folders can be worn in belt pouches that are much shorter and more comfortable to wear than a sheathed fixed blade knife. Folders also don't attract nearly as much attention as a fixed blade knife and can often pass without comment. If, for whatever reason, you fear that the discovery of a knife on your person might cause you problems, opt for a folding knife.

Folders, however, also have their share of disadvantages. As noted earlier, opening a folder requires two separate actions: retrieving the knife from its carry position and opening the blade to the locked position. This is obviously a slower process than simply drawing a sheath knife. As we'll see later, however, with a proper carry and a little practice, you can easily bring your folder into action in less than two seconds.

A more important disadvantage that folders have is that they tend to be weaker than fixed blade knives. You'll recall that one of the absolute requirements of a defensive knife is strength. No matter how skilled you are, Murphy's Law is always lurking out there. If that open shot to your attacker's stomach happens to hit his belt buckle, your knife must be able to withstand the impact without breaking. With fixed blades, the concern is that the blade will break or chip. While this also applies to folders, a bigger concern is that the impact will override the locking system and the blade will close on your fingers. If you choose to carry a folder, invest in one with a rock-solid locking design.

The most traditional and often seen locking system is the rocker lock. With this design, the tang of the blade has a notch milled into it. In the back of the knife's handle, there is a pivoting bar with a lug that fits tightly into the blade notch when the knife is opened. The rear end of the bar is supported by the constant upward pressure of a flat spring, thus the lug end of the bar exerts a constant downward pressure. When the knife is opened, this pressure forces the locking lug into the blade notch and keeps it there to lock the knife open. Closing the knife is accomplished by pushing down on the rear of the pivoting bar (against the spring pressure) and raising the locking lug out of the blade notch.

As long as this design is well executed, it is adequately strong for a personal defense knife. Shop for knives of this design carefully.

This photo shows three rocker-locked folding knives with locking bars of different lengths. The length of the locking bar and placement of the release greatly affect a knife's handling characteristics and blade lockup.

Open and close them repeatedly to see how securely they lock up. Grasp the open blade and try to move it in all directions. Any minor movement during this test could mean a major failure in a fight. Look at the mating of the back of the blade and the locking bar and avoid knives with any visible gap at this point. Make sure the spring is stout and not easily overridden by pressure on the back of the blade. Finally, the locking bars on knives of this design can vary from full length to only half the length of the handle and can feature either recessed or protruding release levers. Grasp the knife in a fighting grip and make sure that no part of your hand is applying pressure to the release that could cause the knife to unlock in a fight. Again, the cost of failure could be a few fingers.

One excellent locking system for folding fighting knives is the liner lock. Originally only used in light-duty pocketknives, in recent years this design has been beefed up considerably and made with state-of-the-art materials, resulting in some tremendously strong folding knives.

In a liner lock knife, one of the liners of the knife's handle is split and a portion of it bowed inward. When the knife is opened, this section of the liner snaps into the handle cavity and butts up against the tang of the blade. This literally blocks the blade from folding into the handle. To close the knife, the

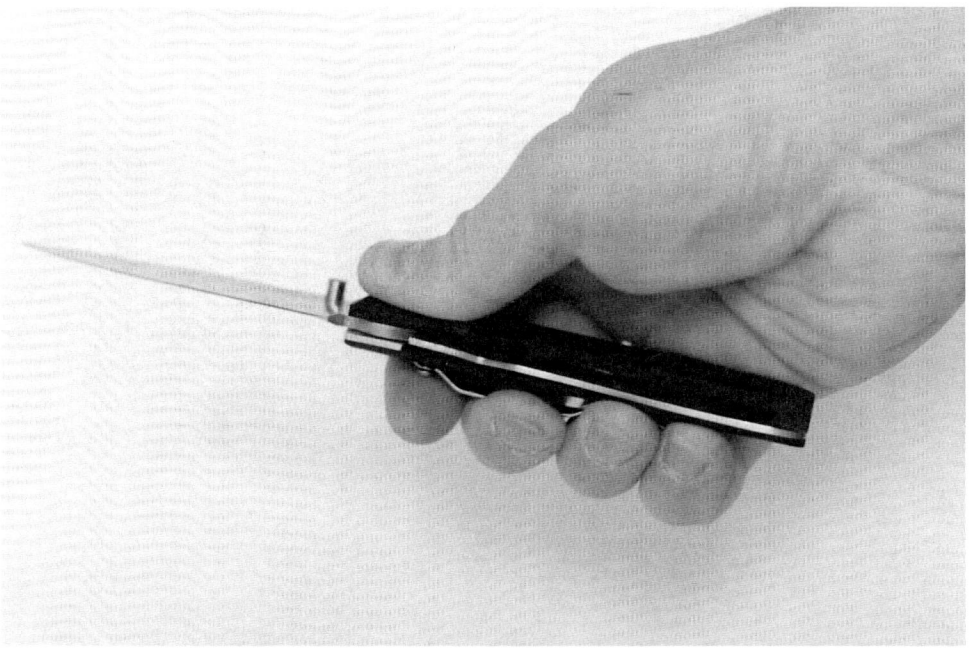

A liner lock actually blocks the closing of the blade and is a good choice in a defensive folding knife. This excellent liner lock folder represents a combined effort by custom makers Bud Nealy and Allen Elishewitz and is one of the author's favorite carry knives.

liner is pushed outward, clearing the way for the blade to fold into the handle.

When shopping for liner lock knives, you must again pay close attention to the sturdiness of the lockup. Any movement or play in the open position should disqualify a knife from use as a defensive blade. Additionally, since there is no backspring on these knives to retain the blade in the handle in the closed position, it is possible that they can open accidentally. Reaching into a pocket and finding your knife partially open is a decidedly unpleasant experience and a very poor way to go into a fight. Some liner lock designs have a detent feature incorporated in the liner and blade which helps keep the blade in the closed position, but many still do not. Avoid liner lock knives that use what looks like a shackle or lanyard ring attached to the butt to hold the blade closed. These can either work loose in the pocket or prevent you from opening your knife when you really need it.

One unique type of locking folding knife is the Filipino *balisong*, or butterfly knife. This type of knife has two independently moveable handles that rotate in opposite directions around the blade, completely enclosing it in the closed position and completely exposing it in the open position. These knives have no springs. Instead, the blade is locked open by pressure of the two handles against a steel pin in the tang of the blade. This creates a three-point locking system which prevents movement of the blade in either direction.

In addition to strength, the balisong offers several other major advantages. First, the unique twin-handle design allows the knife to be opened very quickly in a variety of ways with only one hand. Second, since the handles completely cover the blade in the closed position, a double-edged blade can be used on the knife and it can still be safely carried in the pocket. Finally, the handles of the balisong are shallower than those of other folding knives and the overall design is simpler, making the knife easier to clean and maintain.

Unfortunately, the use of the balisong in movies and on television has caused it to be viewed exactly like switchblades were in the 1950s. It is therefore considered by many authorities to *be* a type of switchblade, making the discovery of one concealed on your person a problem in many jurisdictions. Again, the choice is up to you, as only you will suffer the consequences. I carried a balisong daily for more than 10 years in more than a dozen countries, both in military uniform and civilian clothes, and never had a problem. There's something to be said about being discreet.

If you're shopping for a balisong, the same general guidelines apply as for other folding knives. Look for quality of construction and strength. The popularity of the balisong in the 1980s prompted many cheap versions of the knife to be imported, most of which should not be trusted in a fight. The best commercial balisongs are made by Benchmade Knives of Clackamas, Oregon. This company offers a wide variety of models at a wide variety of prices. Their production models can usually be found for around $50 and are very serviceable knives. Their custom models can easily cost as much or more than a good pistol but are rivaled only by the balisongs made by custom knifemakers.

The idea of a one-handed folding knife is, of course, not a new one. Switchblades, or as they are now popularly known, automatic knives, have been around for over a century. Gravity knives, which are basically springless switchblades that open on the principle of gravity or inertia, also have a long history. The resurgence of interest in these knives and one-handed knives in general has also prompted modern designers and custom cutlers to produce some very unique one-handed openers. In fact, there are probably more one-handed knife designs available today than ever before.

The temptation to purchase one of these nifty gadgets and carry it for self-defense is strong. Thanks to movies and television, there is a widespread belief that the snap of a switchblade will turn even the most determined mugger's spine to jelly and end the confrontation without bloodshed. *This is not the case.* The reality is that many attackers will not even break stride if you pull a knife. Thus, if you carry a knife for self-defense, it must possess the attributes to function as an effective weapon, and you must be prepared to use it as such.

In order to open reliably, many automatic knives must be made with sloppy tolerances. A loose blade will fly open consistently every time the button is pushed but will not stand up to the abuse of full power slashes and stabs against a firm target. The bottom line remains that no matter how attractive or unique a knife design may be, the basic criteria (blade length, blade shape, strength, and deployability) still apply.

With that said, I'll admit that there are automatic knives and nonstandard designs out there that are well-suited for use as personal defense weapons. The secret to finding the one that's right for you is to shop around, look for the best quality you can afford, and be discriminating in your choice. Ultimately, you're betting your life on that blade. That's a bet I wouldn't take lightly.

CHAPTER 3

Carry Options for Fixed Blade Knives

Straight bladed knives offer the greatest variety of carry options for personal defense. Throughout history, people of different cultures have carried knives of this type in virtually every position imaginable. Their carry choices, predictably, were influenced primarily by their everyday dress and habits. Some of these carry methods, for better or worse, have been adopted and promoted by modern knife makers and users.

The fictional exploits of various heroes and villains have also led to the popularity, at least in theory, of various methods of carrying edged weapons. In most cases, however, these carries are only as realistic as the fanciful stories in which they appear and are not practical or comfortable for everyday wear.

In this chapter, we'll take a hard look at the various methods of carrying a straight blade and the advantages and disadvantages of each. We'll also examine the proper tactics for each of these carries that will allow you deploy your knife quickly while minimizing exposure to your opponent's attack. The first consideration when carrying any type of straight blade knife, however, should be a good sheath.

Sheaths for personal defense knives must do five basic things: protect the user from the knife edges and point; retain the knife securely; expose enough of the handle so the

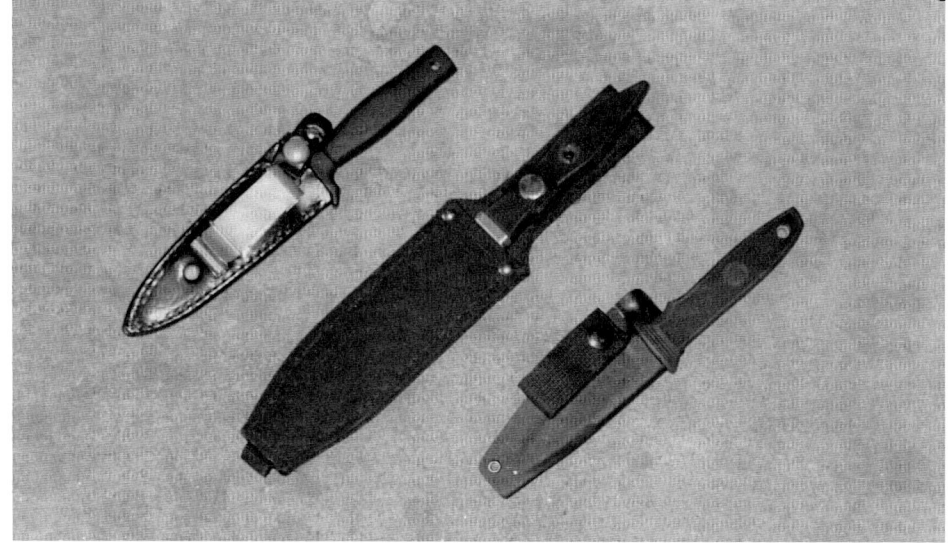

Most knife sheaths today are made from leather, Cordura nylon, or Kydex plastic. Attachment systems include spring steel clips, belt loops for overt belt carry, and belt loops for inside-the-pants carry.

A typical leather friction-fit sheath, here with the A.G. Russell "Sting" knife. Friction-fit sheaths do not work well for inverted carries and typically leave very little of the knife handle available for gripping during a draw.

hand can get a solid, reasonably complete grip before drawing; release the knife easily during the draw; and present the knife in a position where it can be drawn easily.

Any quality sheath should protect you from the sharp edges and point of your blade. If a sheath doesn't meet this basic requirement, it's not much of a sheath. Leather, Cordura nylon, and a heat moldable plastic called Kydex are the most popular sheath materials and, when properly utilized, all provide adequate protection. In some cases, sheaths can also be fabricated from metal, wood, Micarta, plastic, and other rigid substances. While these materials provide excellent protection from the blade's edge and point, they can be bulkier and heavier than standard sheaths.

A good sheath must also retain the knife so it doesn't come out until you want it to. When you are ready to draw the knife, the sheath should expose enough of the handle to allow you to grip the knife firmly before you draw and should release the knife smoothly and easily.

The simplest method of accomplishing this is a *friction fit*, in which the sheath is molded closely to the form of the knife so the friction of the sheath material against the blade and handle is sufficient to retain the knife. This is normally seen with leather sheaths and is adequate for carry styles that place the knife handle upright. Leather friction sheaths are not secure enough for inverted carries, however. Since the handle of the knife must be mostly exposed to offer an immediate grip, a leather sheath cannot apply enough pressure to the blade and hilt to retain the knife securely. Keep in mind that the fit of a knife in a friction fit sheath tends to loosen with age and exposure to moisture. Watch for this and be prepared to replace your sheath if you notice excessive wear.

Kydex sheaths offer a significant improvement over leather when it comes to molded sheaths. This relatively rigid material can be heat molded around the contours of a knife handle or guard so once the form of the sheath is established, it will retain that shape practically indefinitely. This provides a much more secure hold on the knife. Kydex sheaths can even be designed to incorporate release tabs which are pressed with the thumb of the knife hand to relieve some of the pressure on the knife and speed up the draw. An additional bonus is the fact that Kydex does not absorb moisture like leather or nylon. This is an important consideration for personal defense knives worn close to the body where perspiration could soak into the sheath material and possibly cause your blade to rust. The only disadvantages to Kydex sheaths are that they can sometimes scratch your knife blade and that they tend to be noisier than leather or nylon.

Another common method of retaining a knife in its sheath is the use of retaining straps. These are usually found on leather and Cordura sheaths and consist of a strap with a snap fastener that wraps around the guard or handle of the knife to hold it in place. The best designs of this type have a strap that goes over or across one quillon of the guard and feature a quick-release "thumb-break" snap like that found on pistol holsters. Avoid sheaths with retaining straps that encircle the handle, since they typically offer poor

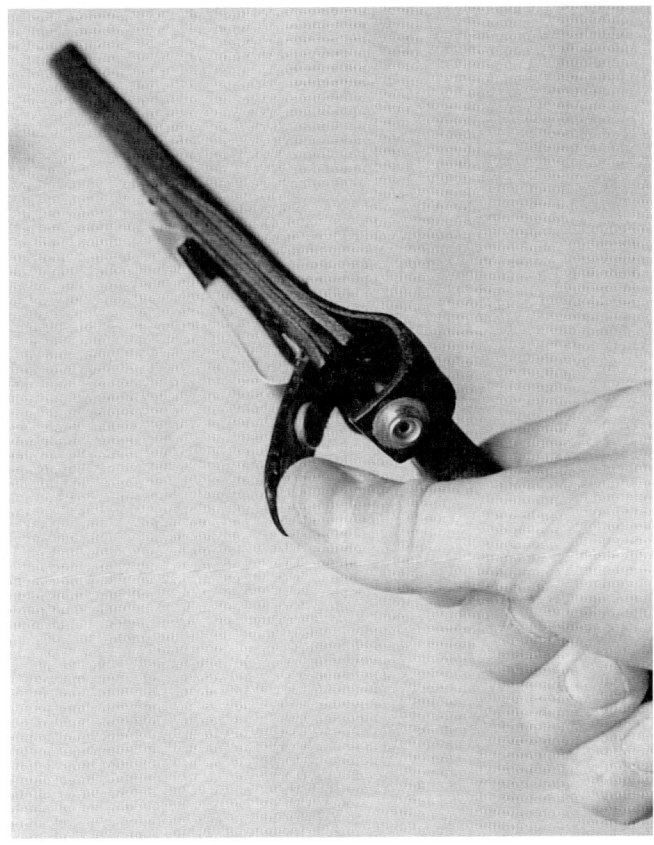

Thumb-break sheaths, such as this one for the Gerber MKI, offer a good compromise between security and speed of deployment.

security and are difficult to release in a hurry. There are a variety of other sheath designs commercially available which incorporate unique retention and release systems. These range from simple spring clips to sophisticated push-button mechanisms. Although some of these designs have merit, many of them are simply gimmicks that can't be counted on to hold onto your knife or release it when you need it.

One of the most unique retention systems I've seen was designed by custom knifemaker Bud Nealy. It employs four gold-plated rare earth magnets set into a Kydex sheath. The pull of these exceptionally powerful magnets against the steel blade is sufficient to retain the knife securely in the sheath, even in the inverted

Sheaths made of Kydex, a moldable thermoplastic sheet, offer very good retention and a straightforward draw stroke. Shown here is a Kydex sheath made by Cutlery Shoppe with their excellent Gryphon M10 boot knife.

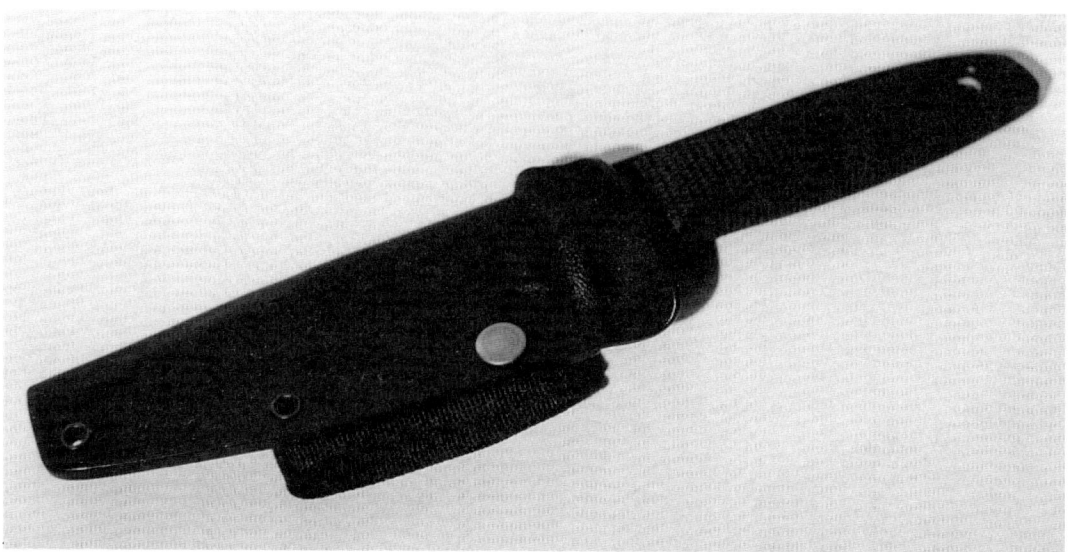

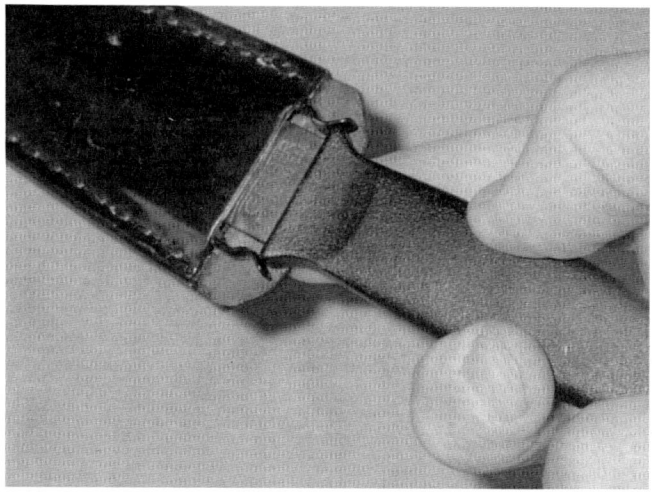

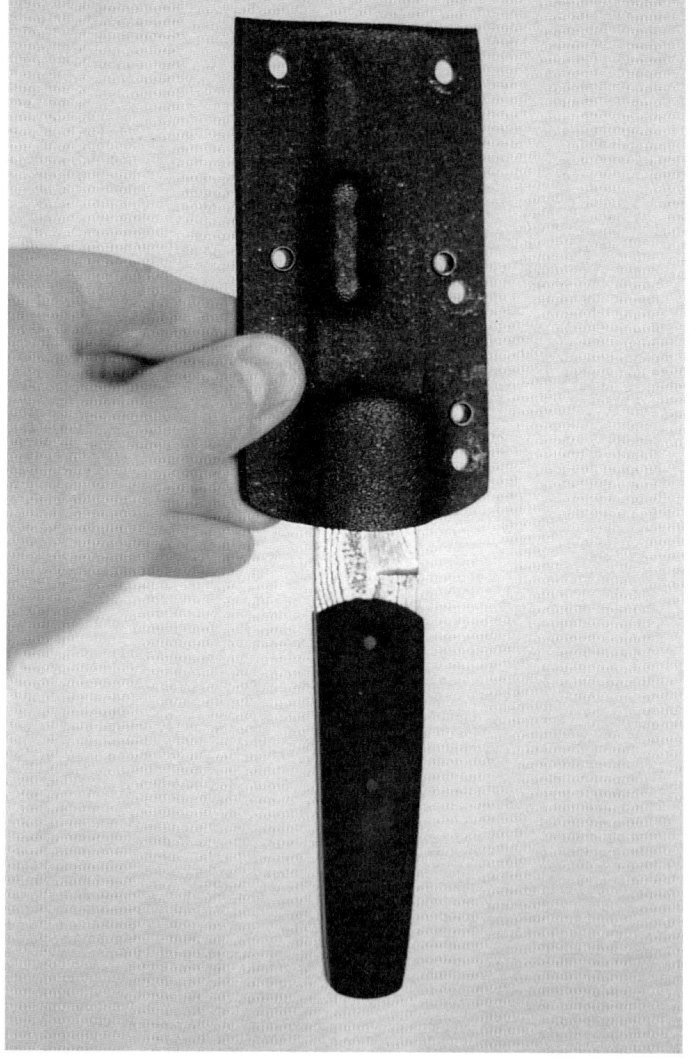

The original production Gerber Guardian, designed by knife maker Robert Loveless, featured a unique spring retention system that gripped the knife's guard. Newer production models feature a solid plastic sheath with an adjustable tension release, but overall quality is not as good as the originals.

Custom knife maker Bud Nealy's Multi-Concealment System (MCS) features a unique Kydex sheath, which incorporates three powerful rare earth magnets to retain the knife. The power of these magnets is shown here as they retain the blade, even though it is only partially inserted in the sheath. Nealy's sheaths offer the fastest draw of any Kydex sheaths the author has seen.

Carry Options for Fixed Blade Knives

Bud Nealy's Multi-Concealment Sheath system is the most comprehensive approach to concealed knife carry available. It consists of a superbly designed Kydex sheath mated with mounting hardware that allows for comfortable carry in a wide variety of positions. Nealy's knives are available in several styles and blade lengths, and craftsmanship is strictly first class. Shown here (with all mounting hardware) is his Aikuchi model with a damascus steel blade and neoprene handle slabs.

Left: Bud Nealy's unique Pesh-Kabz (Travel Knife) with a Micarta handle. Like all Nealy's knives, it comes complete with his MCS system and all carry attachments.

Above: Bud Nealy's Aikuchi with a damascus blade and his Kwaito with a stainless steel blade and G-10 handle slabs. Both are shown with their unique MCS sheaths configured for breast pocket and neck carry, respectively.

position. A firm pull on the handle of the knife frees the blade smoothly and more quickly than any other design I've tried. Best of all, this superb sheath is supplied with a variety of Kydex mounting hardware, allowing the knife to be carried comfortably in many different positions (these will be examined in detail later). Nealy offers this sheath and accessories with three different knife designs: the *Aikuchi*, which features a Japanese-style chisel point; the *Kinzhal*, with a symmetrically tapered blade profile; and the *Pesh-Kabz* (Travel Knife), which boasts an ingenious blade grind that combines the cutting ability of a deep hollow grind with the strength of an armor-piercing point. All three knives come in a choice of two blade lengths as part of this maker's Multi-Concealment Sheath (MCS) system, one of the most versatile personal defense knife packages available. The workmanship of Mr. Nealy's sheaths and knives is in a class by itself, and his designs exhibit real-world practicality seldom seen in the knife trade. Amazingly, his knives remain some of the most affordable custom cutlery available.

The final requirement of a good sheath is that it must present the knife in a position where it can be drawn easily. This goes back to the concept of deployability and is where we really get into the specifics of the many ways knives can be carried. These modes of carry not only have intrinsic advantages and disadvantages of their own, they also tend to work better with some knives and sheaths than others. The only way to find out what really works is to try every design you can lay your hands on and decide for yourself.

When examining a knife/sheath combination for a specific mode of carry, keep in mind that you must be able to draw the knife quickly from a variety of positions, preferably with either hand. Try the knife out wearing the clothes you would normally wear on a day-to-day basis. If you're uncertain about how the knife will carry when you are wearing something special from your wardrobe, go change into those clothes and try it again.

Some consideration should also be given to the ease with which the knife can be replaced in its sheath. Ideally, you should be able to put the knife back quickly and unobtrusively. That way, when entering areas or situations where the danger of attack is high, you can draw your knife and have it discreetly ready in your hand. When the danger has passed, you can then quietly put the knife away without anyone being the wiser.

With a little bit of charm and effort, you might be able to develop a special relationship with a knife dealer in your area and borrow knives for a day or two before buying. This will allow you to take them home and try them out with everything in your wardrobe. It also makes it possible for you to practice draws from concealment away from the prying eyes of other customers. I was lucky enough to have this arrangement when I first started buying defensive knives. I learned a lot about different knives and avoided wasting money on a number of designs that looked great in the showcase but carried terribly. By the way, if the dealer is hesitant to go for such a deal, offering a deposit often helps.

One final bit of advice when shopping for and trying out personal defense knives—in addition to trying draws from different positions with both hands, *try drawing the knife while moving.* Specifically, try draws while running forward, backpedaling, and sidestepping. If you get attacked before you can get your knife out, you will have to buy time and distance to execute your draw. Many people ignore this simple fact and will either be completely unable to draw their blades in a fight because they are on the move or will be sitting ducks while they execute their draw.

Now let's take a critical look at the various carry modes for straight blade knives and the tactics to make the best of each.

OPEN BELT CARRY

This carry is the type normally used with hunting and survival knives when you're out in the woods. You may be surprised to learn that carrying a knife in this manner can be perfectly legal in many populated areas as well. Since you are announcing to the world that you have a knife, everyone who has a problem with that can stay away from you, and the authorities know up front that you are armed.

On the positive side, this carry mode allows for the carry of rather large knives and provides good access with either hand. The open display of a knife can also intimidate many would-be attackers who prefer to prey upon unarmed victims.

The downside of this carry is that its conspicuousness could cause you problems in certain areas, such as restaurants, banks, malls, and other places that are open to the public but are technically private property. The legality of this carry is also usually limited to sporting and hunting style knives, making it a poor choice if you prefer a double-edged defensive blade. Knives carried in sheaths hung vertically from the belt tend to ride up and poke you in the ribs when you sit down and, for this same reason, are very slow to draw from a seated position. Finally, although the open carry of a knife might intimidate some people, other attackers might decide that the only safe tactic is to put you down immediately. They may therefore be even more cunning and brutal in their attack, offering you little or no chance of defending yourself.

WAISTBAND/INSIDE-THE-PANTS CARRIES

Carrying a knife on the waistband, with the sheath concealed inside the pants, is a

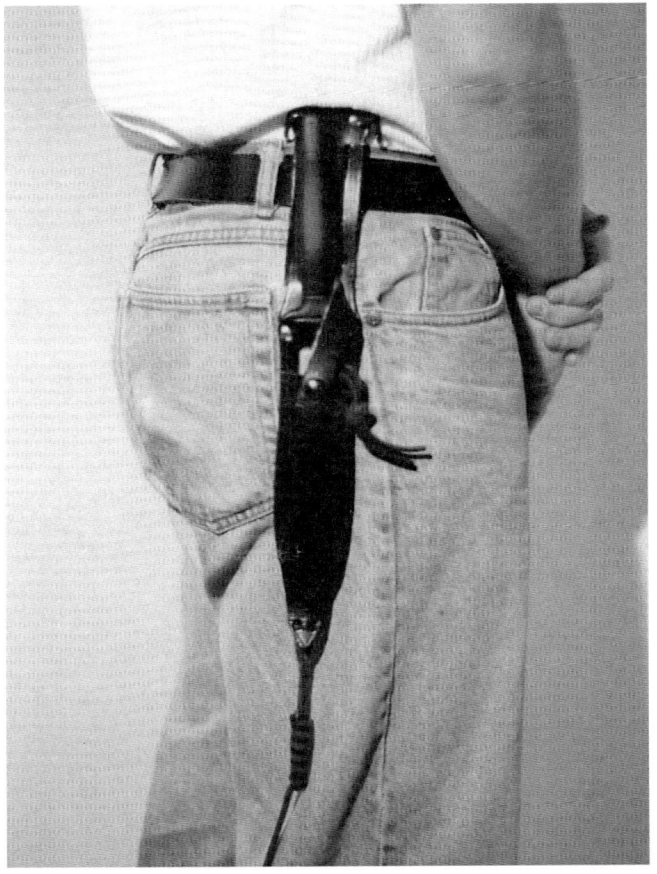

Open belt carry of a fixed blade knife is convenient and perfectly legal in many areas; however, it is not usually well received in places like banks, shopping malls, and college campuses. Its drawbacks also include warning potential attackers that you are armed and being somewhat uncomfortable when seated in a car.

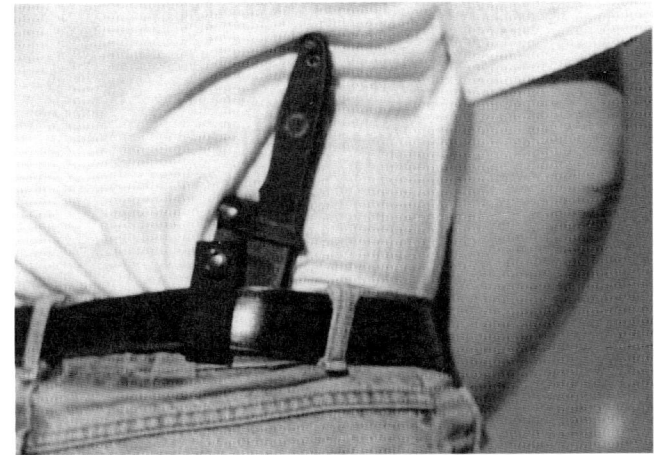

The inside-the-pants carry offers concealability, quick access, and reasonably good comfort. Shown here is Cutlery Shoppe's Gryphon M10 knife with Kydex sheath. Note that the sheath has a snap-fastened belt loop so it can be removed to safely replace the knife or ditch it if a search is imminent.

popular and reasonably versatile carry. Since the knife is on the waist, it is close to the level of the hands and therefore easily accessible and quickly drawn. Boot knives and shorter fighting knives with blades 5 inches long or less can be carried in this position, requiring only a long shirt, sweater, or light jacket to conceal the knife handle, which rides above the pants.

Sheaths suitable for this carry include those equipped with metal spring clips or true inside-the-pants designs featuring a belt loop that extends over the waistband of the pants to loop around the belt. The latter design is more secure, promoting a positive, glitch-free draw. However, a belt *must* be worn with this style of sheath, making it incompatible with some styles of pants. Additionally, since this type of sheath is anchored to the belt, replacing a drawn knife can be a slow, exacting, and sometimes dangerous process. Inside-the-pants sheaths with belt loops that have snap fasteners can be removed from the belt quickly for resheathing the knife (or ditching it) and are therefore preferred.

Sheaths with spring clips do not offer the security of the belt loop styles, and it is not uncommon for these sheaths to remain on the

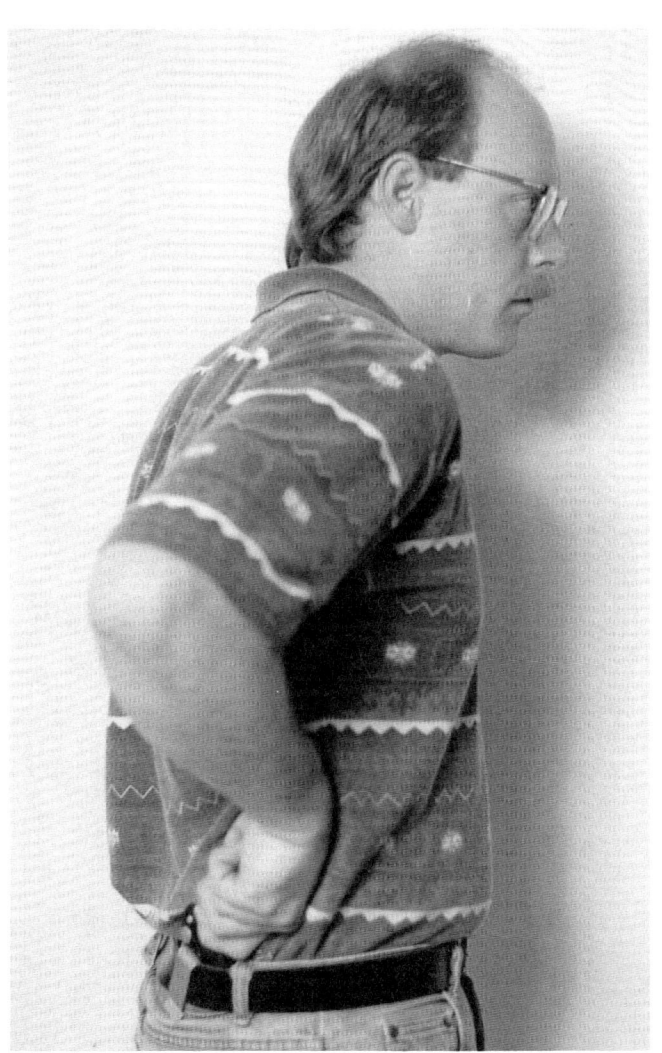
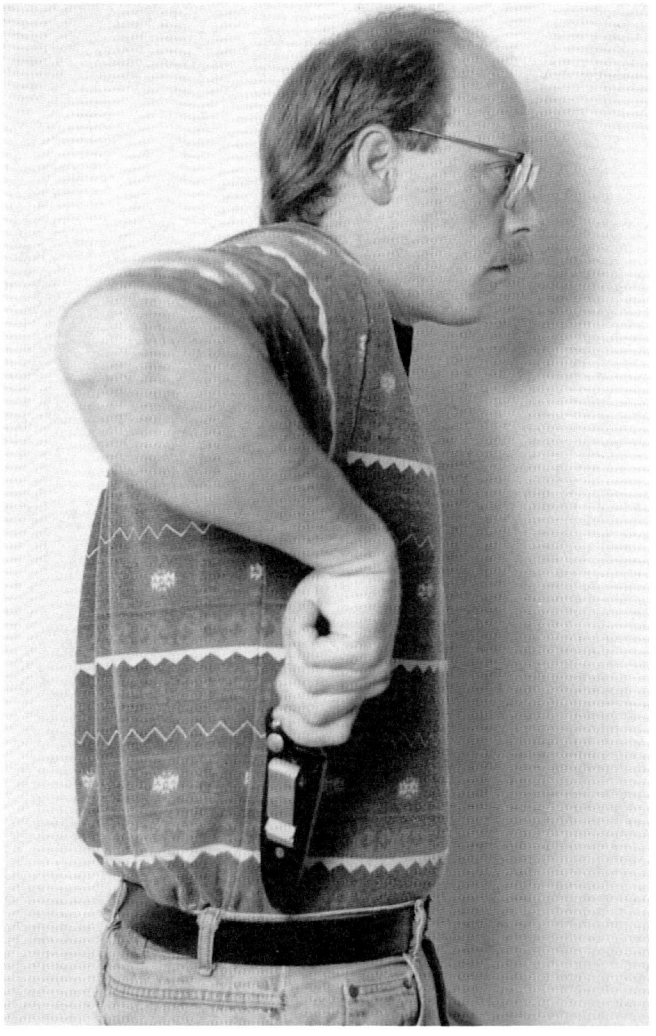

The problem with spring clip sheaths is that they sometimes slip off the belt or waistband during the draw. If this happens, the failure drill is to grasp the sheath with your free hand or teeth and complete the draw stroke to expose your blade.

knife during a fast draw. As such, your drawing practice must incorporate "immediate action" drills not unlike those for firearms that have failed to fire. These consist of grasping the sheath with your free hand or even your teeth to complete the draw and expose your blade.

On the positive side, spring clip sheaths can be worn with any kind of pants, shorts, or, for women, skirts. They can also be easily canted or angled to one side or the other to provide a better position for a draw and to keep the knife handle from jabbing you when you are seated. The fact that these sheaths can be removed from the belt quickly makes putting a drawn knife back in the sheath much easier, as well as allowing you to remove and ditch both knife and sheath if you fear you will be searched.

The greatest disadvantage of inside-the-pants carries is that they require a shirt or jacket for effective concealment. If you are partial to wearing your shirts tucked in, a jacket is a must, even in warm weather. The best compromise I've found with this carry is to wear a jacket or sweater during cool weather and polo shirts with the shirt tails out during warm weather. Buy jackets and

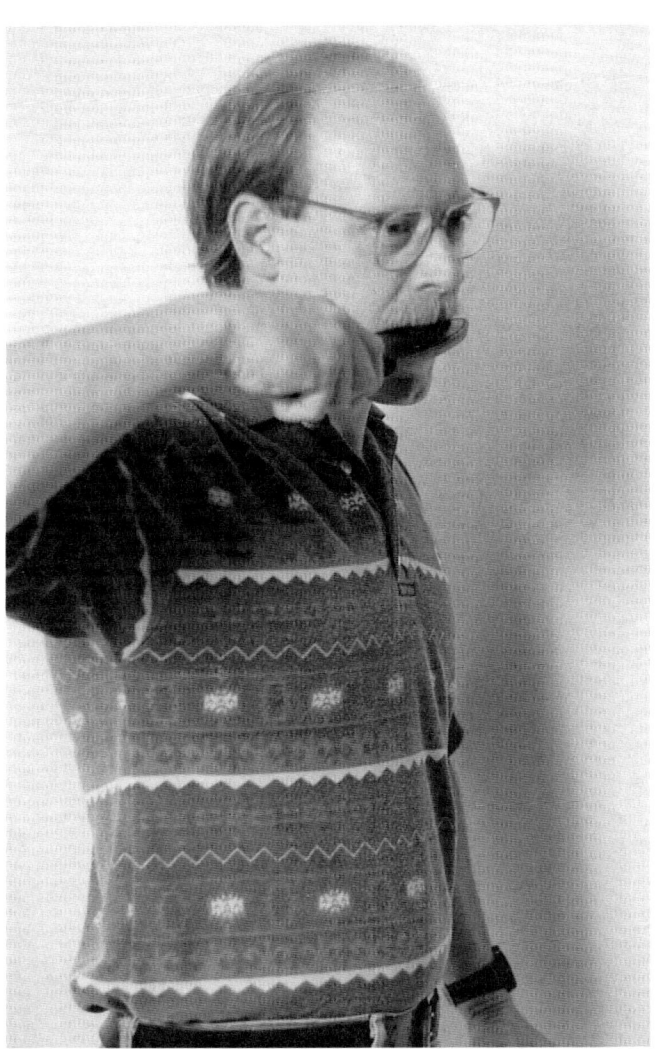

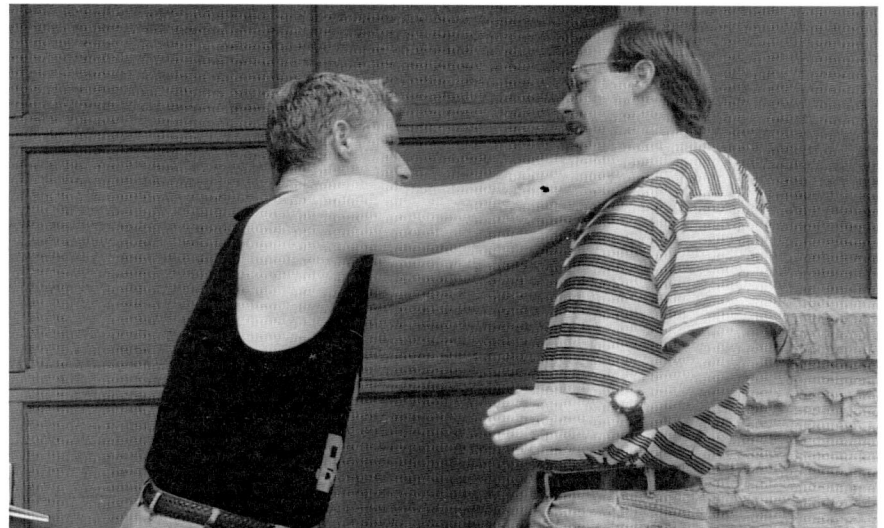

Sometimes an unarmed defense can be performed at the same time you draw your blade. Here a typical "punch and draw" is used to loosen a choke hold and draw a knife from a waistband carry.

shirts that are a bit long to prevent them from riding up over the handle of your knife, and consider buying pants an inch larger in the waist to allow enough room for your knife.

If you opt for a waistband carry, you must decide where on your waistband you will place the knife. The most popular choice is to the rear on the strong-hand side, similar to a so-called "kidney hold" with a pistol. The jacket or shirt is either swept aside or raised by the strong hand as it goes for the handle of the knife. This makes for a fast draw with the strong hand and can be combined with a punch, palm heel strike, or finger jab with the free hand to buy time for the draw. A knife in this position is still accessible to the weak hand by reaching around the back. It can also be drawn from most disadvantaged positions and while running.

The disadvantage of this carry is usually immediately apparent when you sit down. Most knives carried in this position will remind you of their presence with a firm jab in the back. You will also notice that drawing from this carry while seated in a car is not easy, especially if you're wearing a seat belt. This problem can be reduced by tilting the knife away from your spine so it is positioned more diagonally, but be careful that the handle of the knife doesn't "print" or show through your jacket or shirt, since it will tend to stick out from the body more when tilted. Also, be aware when you stand up from a seated position, since knife handles have a habit of catching on the backs of chairs. Sliding forward a bit in your chair before you rise will help avoid this problem.

Another common waistband carry places the knife between the kidneys in the middle of the back. This is more comfortable than the kidney hold when standing and allows for a very quick draw with either hand. This carry provides better concealment as well, since the knife is effectively hidden in the hollow of the lower back. When you sit down, however, this carry suffers from the same problems as the kidney hold, only to a greater degree. Drawing from this position while seated in a car is also virtually impossible.

One custom knifemaker who has taken a fresh and innovative look at concealed carry systems is James S. Piorek, who operates under the highly appropriate business name of "Blade Rigger." One of his sheath designs called the JSP Static-Cord™ System provides an excellent solution to the problem of using a strong side or center-of-the-back inside-the-pants carry while seated in a car. The knife is carried in a

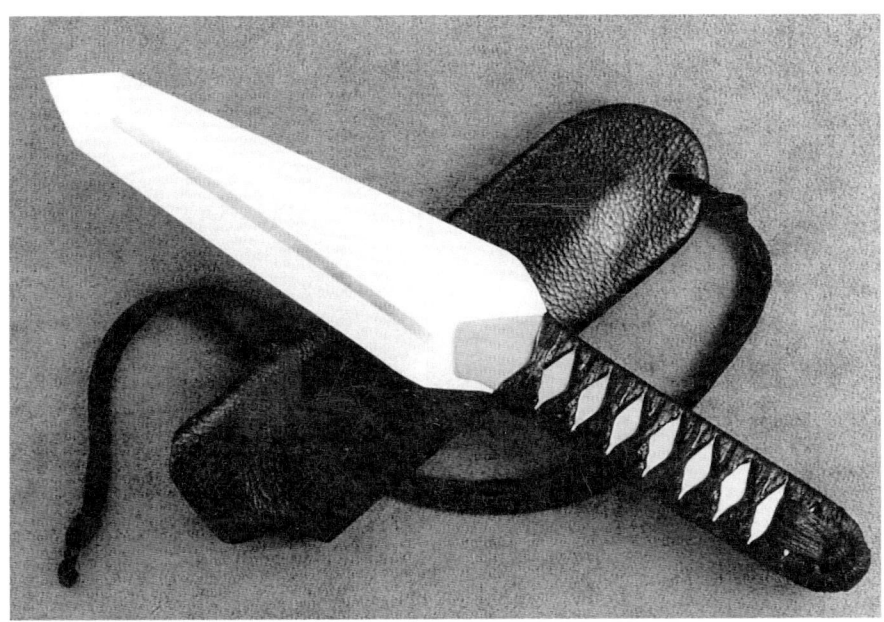

A beautiful chisel ground dagger by custom knife maker James S. Piorek, aka Blade Rigger. Note the cord attached to the sheath which is the heart of his JSP Static Cord™ system.

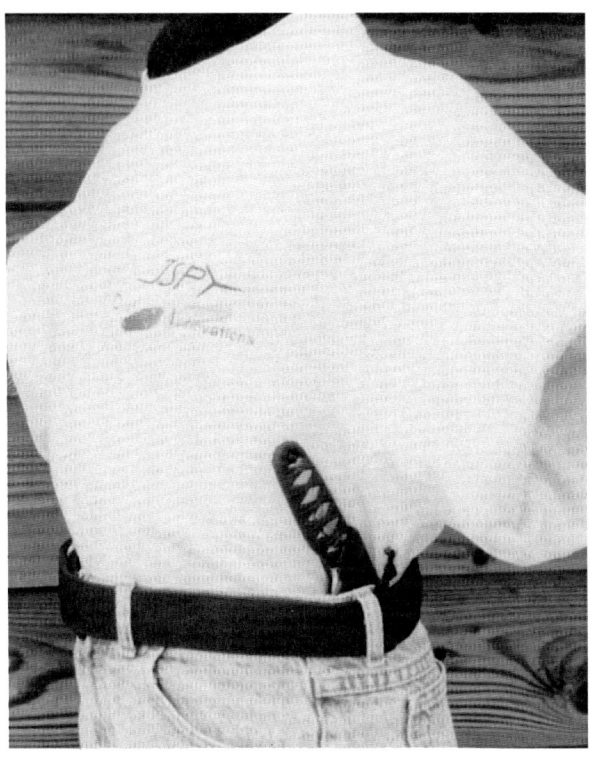 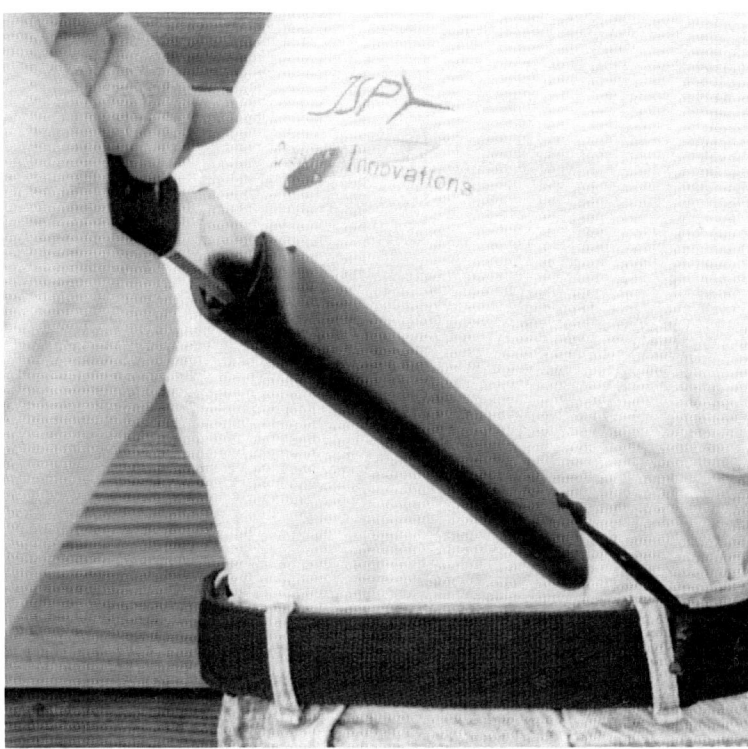

These photos show how the JSP Static Cord™ system allows the sheath to be drawn with the blade. When the cord is fully extended and the sheath is safely away from the body, the knife is released.

leather-laminated Kydex sheath and retained by a cam locking action that eliminates the need for snaps or straps. Attached to the tip of this sheath is a loop of nylon parachute cord about a foot long. This loop is secured to your belt or a belt loop by wrapping it around and passing the sheath through the end of the loop to form a cow hitch knot. The sheath is then inserted into the waistband where it is retained by a friction fit. When you draw the knife, the sheath is withdrawn with it. When it hits the limit of its static-cord loop, the knife pops out and the sheath drops out of the way to your side. The fact that the knife clears the sheath when the sheath is away from the body makes this design a very safe way to deploy a sharp blade.

Since the sheath is initially drawn together with the knife, the draw can be done at a variety of angles—an important advantage when executing a draw in a real world environment. Best of all, when seated in a car, the knife and sheath can be easily removed and placed on the seat next to your right thigh. You can fasten your seat belt normally, yet still have your knife instantly available in the event of a carjacking or similar attack. This unique design, along with the slim profile and contoured edges of the sheath, also makes replacing the knife in its sheath and your waistband a snap.

One unique center-of-the-back carry is accomplished by mounting the sheath horizontally on the belt with the knife handle facing the strong-hand side. This is a very comfortable carry, even when seated, and makes for a very fast draw with the strong hand. The problems with this carry are that it is really only practical with short knives and, unless you are thin or flexible enough to reach all the way around your waist from the front or back, the knife is practically inaccessible to the weak hand. This carry also requires an extra long coat or shirt for good

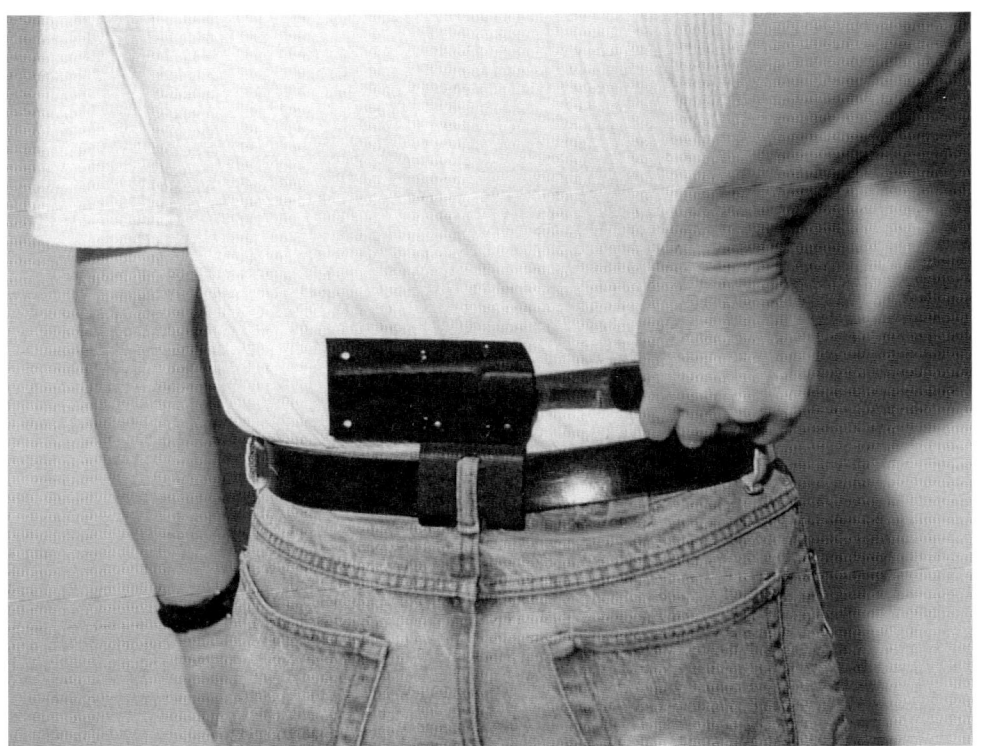

Carrying a fixed blade knife horizontally on the belt can be very comfortable and concealable but may limit your draw to your strong hand only. Shown here is a horizontal carry using Bud Nealy's MCS. Note that the mounting hardware allows the knife to ride above the belt line for better concealment under a short jacket.

concealment since no part of the knife is hidden within the pants.

One exception to this rule is the work of custom knifemaker Bud Nealy, whom I mentioned earlier. His Kydex sheaths are provided with a horizontal belt attachment which places the knife *above* the line of the belt to ensure good concealment. If your coat or shirt rides up, the knife and sheath will still remain concealed. With this sheath, like all belt-mounted sheaths, I recommend that you purchase a sturdy leather belt as wide as the belt loops on the sheath. This will ensure that the sheath and knife are securely anchored and will not slide or move during a quick draw. Leather pistol belts are the best for this purpose, but any thick leather belt of the correct width will suffice.

The V-Stat™ system by James S. Piorek takes a very innovative approach to the horizontal carry. It consists of a Velcro-covered panel that attaches to the back of the belt with an integral belt loop. The panel is wisely designed so that it works equally well mounted above or below the belt. A generous strip of matching Velcro material is securely sewn to the outside leather lamination of the Kydex knife sheath so the sheath can be attached to the panel at any angle the wearer prefers. The use of a leather covering is attractive and provides a noiseless surface over the inherently noisy Kydex. The sheath is then further secured with an optional quick-release retention strap in conjunction with Piorek's JSP Static-Cord™ described earlier. Although the former arrangement is slightly faster on the draw, the static cord makes resheathing the knife much safer and easier since it can be done away from your body.

Piorek also offers his Spinal Backup II™ system, which consists of a Velcro-covered panel which is secured between a shoulder harness assembly and the rear of the belt so it lies directly over the lower spine. A knife sheath covered with matching Velcro is attached to this panel so the handle faces downward and is available for an immediate draw. This design allows the draw angle to be

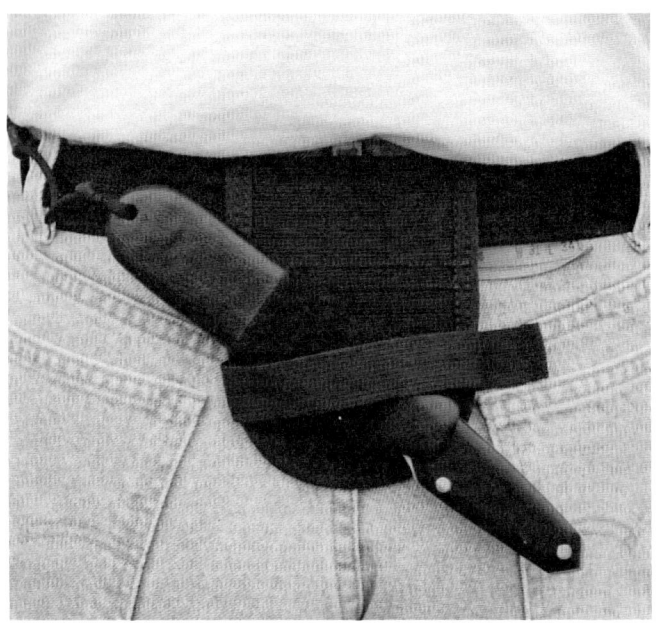 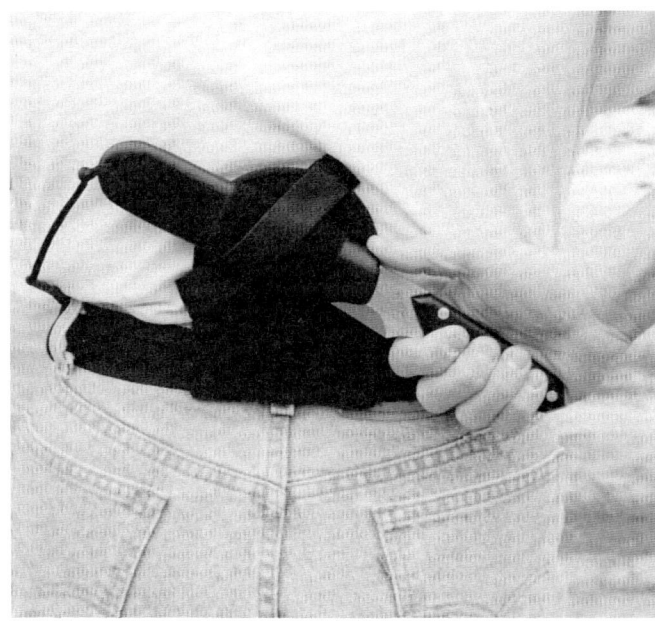

Shown here is James S. Piorek's V-Stat™ belt carry system worn above and below the belt. The choice of carry would depend on the length of the jacket or shirt worn over the rig. The Velcro fixtures on this design allow the knife to be positioned at virtually any angle for a comfortable draw. It can also be used in conjunction with the aforementioned Static Cord system.

adjusted to the wearer's preference and can be used to effectively conceal very long knives or even short swords.

Knives carried on the waistband or belt can also be positioned in the crossdraw position. This means that they are placed on the weak-hand side of the body and that the strong hand must reach across the body to execute a draw.

Since knives carried in this way must be positioned farther forward to be within reach of the opposite hand, concealment is more difficult than with other waistband carries. However, this carry is much more comfortable than belt carries with the knife positioned at the back and allows a speedy draw with either hand, even when seated in a vehicle. Additionally, this carry position allows you to draw your knife discreetly with a simple arm-crossing movement. This can be a great advantage if you anticipate trouble but haven't progressed to the full combat mode yet.

You should note that the standard waistband and belt carries are most compatible with a standard grip draw and have been described as such. In other words, when you grip the knife for a draw, the blade will protrude from the index finger side of the hand. If your personal knife-fighting style favors a reverse grip (a grip with the blade extending from the little finger side of the hand), you can still use these carries but you'll have to adapt your body mechanics a bit to develop a smooth drawing technique. The belt carry positions best suited for reverse-grip draws are the horizontal carry, the crossdraw carry, and the strong-side carry. As you'll see later, there are some distinct advantages to the reverse grip when retrieving your knife discreetly, so even if you prefer fighting with a standard grip, practice in reverse-grip draws is a good idea.

BOOT CARRIES

One of the most popular knife carries among fictional characters is the boot carry,

The Piorek Spinal Backup II™ is a very unusual system that carries the knife inverted at the small of the back through the use of a shoulder harness. This system can be used to conceal very large blades, including short swords, very effectively.

wherein a nasty character conceals an equally nasty piece of steel in the top of his boot. When the plot demands, he slyly reaches down and withdraws the knife to carry out his evil deeds.

This looks great on TV, but it doesn't work so well in the cold, cruel world of reality.

Before I continue, let me first clarify the term "boot knife." Originally, this term referred to small (and sometimes not so small) knives carried in sheaths secured in high-top boots. These boots were worn *outside* one's pants to provide protection against mud, rocks, and other detritus routinely encountered before paved streets became common. These boots typically reached just below the knee and provided an ideal place to carry a knife. With a slight crouch, you could bring your hand down to calf level and quickly retrieve your blade. Keep in mind that during this period of history (basically, the latter half of the 19th century), carrying a knife or even a gun was common practice in many areas, so concealment was not a great concern.

Today, the term boot knife is used to describe an entire category of fixed blade personal defense knives, which typically average 9 inches or less in length. In most cases, these knives have sheaths equipped with spring steel clips (often called "boot clips"), which are theoretically designed to allow the sheath to be secured to the top of a boot. These knives are usually designed with fighting in mind and typically meet the criteria for a personal defense knife prescribed earlier. The carry of these knives, however, is certainly not limited to tucking them into a cowboy boot. In fact, this is probably one of the least used methods of carry for these knives, and for good reason.

The high-top boots which originally inspired boot knives are rarely seen these days. If someone did choose to wear them, the sight of a knife handle poking out of one of them would probably draw some attention, especially from the police.

The styles of boots that are popular today include cowboy boots, jack boots, combat boots, and ankle-high dress and hiking boots. These boots are commonly worn with pants rather than shorts and, in most cases, the pant legs are worn outside the boots. Thus, a boot knife worn at the top of one of these styles of boot is anywhere from 6 inches to a full foot lower than one worn in traditional knee-high boots and is covered by a pant leg. While this situation makes for effective concealment, it does not promote a quick draw. The pant leg must be raised above the handle of the knife, which, for some boots, means all the way up to the knee. This normally requires two hands and requires that you either fall to the ground, hop on one foot, or bend over and place your

The problem with the conventional upright boot knife carry is that with many boot styles, the pant leg must be raised nearly to the knee to clear the knife. Obviously this would be a difficult task when the bad guys are closing quickly.

head within easy kicking range of your opponent's feet. None of these are particularly desirable in a street attack situation.

If you insist on using a boot carry, the best solution is to suspend your knife upside down from your boot top so drawing is accomplished by reaching under your pant leg and pulling the knife downward. Bud Nealy's Multi-Concealment System comes with sheath hardware specifically designed for this type of carry, as does the revamped design of Gerber's Guardian boot knife. Concealment for this style of carry is most effective with pants made of heavy materials, such as denim, or pants that fit loosely around the calf, such as "boot cut" styles. Knives will print through tight pants and pants made of light material. Also, make sure you buy pants long enough to cover the handle of your knife even when you're sitting or have your legs crossed. If necessary, buy your pants extra long and have the hems tailored to the right length.

Carry Options for Fixed Blade Knives

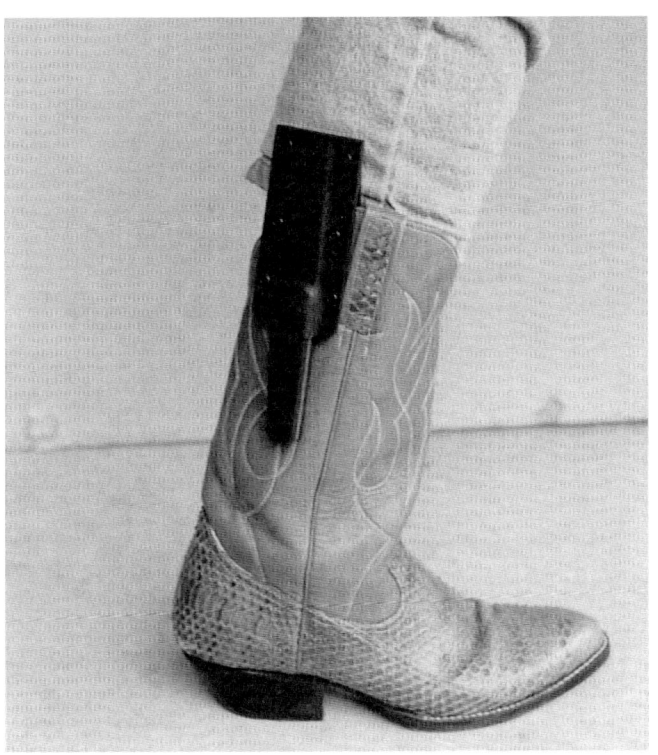
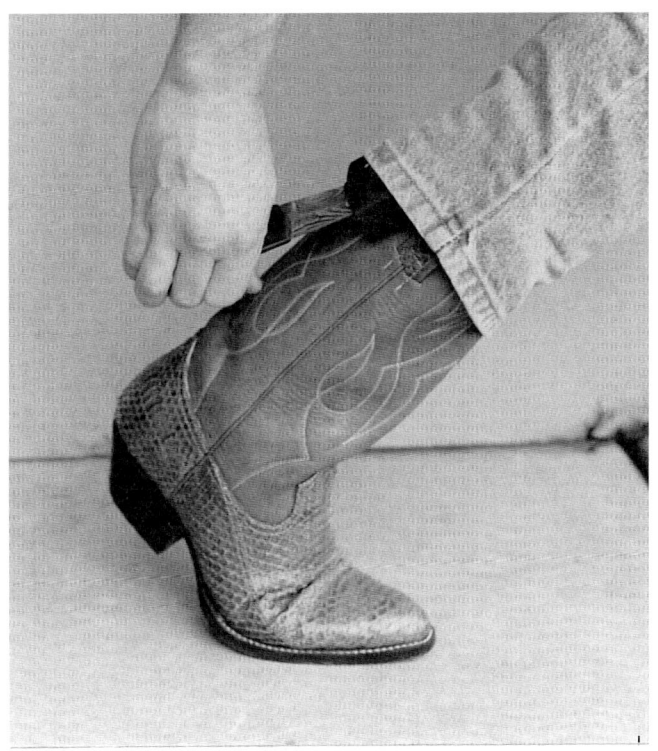

With cowboy boots or other high-topped boot styles, an inverted boot carry is best. This allows the knife handle to point downward yet remain concealed by the pant leg. Reaching under the pant leg gives instant access to the knife and allows for a surprisingly quick draw. Here this carry and draw are demonstrated with a Bud Nealy Aikuchi and MCS sheath with boot clip mounting.

The upright boot knife carry works reasonably well with ankle-high boots since the pant leg does not need to be raised very high to clear the knife. This carry can be a bit uncomfortable, however. Note here that the spring clip of the knife sheath is exposed on the outside of the boot. Securing the knife with matching patches of Velcro inside the boot and on the back of the sheath would offer a lower profile.

If you like the boot carry but sometimes wear shoes rather than boots, all is not lost. You can effectively replace your boot top with an elastic knee support available from sports stores and most pharmacies. Wear this support around your calf at the same height as your boot top and attach your knife sheath to it instead.

If you normally wear long pants, the handle-up style of boot knife carry is only practical with ankle-high boots. With these boots, you need only raise your pant leg about eight inches to clear the knife to be drawn.

Although knives with boot clip sheaths can be used with ankle-high boots, they don't offer very good security and can come loose if you walk or climb a flight of stairs too quickly. A better method is to glue or sew a generous patch of Velcro into your boot (the woolly loop piece) and attach a matching piece (the plastic hook piece) to the back of your sheath. The Velcro will keep your knife securely in place and provides for a more certain draw than a knife with a boot clip sheath.

I've found that ankle-high dress boots (aka "Beatle Boots" for you rock-and-roll trivia fans) offer the best platform for handle-up boot knife carries since there is usually some space between the boot and your leg. Lace-up hiking boots, though more fashionable, fit tightly around the ankle and tend to draw the handle of my knife into painful contact with my ankle bone. Very slender knives work better with boots of this type, as well as with military-style combat boots. Extra-long pants are a must with this carry, however, since raising your pant leg even slightly could expose your blade.

As with the handle-down carry, the handle-up carry is adaptable for use when wearing shoes rather than boots. Instead of a knee support, get an elastic ankle support the same color as your socks. Then clip or Velcro your knife sheath onto the ankle support in the same position you use for the boot carry.

One final option for boot knife carry is to have a pair of boots made or customized so they incorporate a knife sheath into the upper section of the boot. Depending upon the height of the boot, the sheath can either be built into the top rim or the side of the boot. This is generally much more secure than an add-on sheath and offers a much flatter concealment profile. If you choose a knife that matches the color of your boots, this carry can be practically invisible. Additionally, when compared to other forms of custom tailoring, such as adding knife pockets to every pair of pants you own, the price of one or two pairs of custom boots becomes a real bargain. If you choose to give this method a try, make sure that the leather used by the cobbler is thick enough to keep the knife blade from poking through. You might consider having a simple Kydex sheath made first and then having that built into your boots.

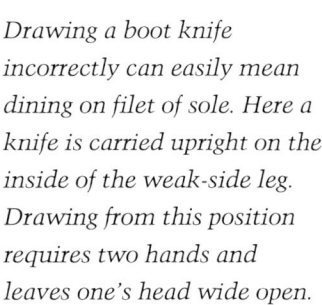

Drawing a boot knife incorrectly can easily mean dining on filet of sole. Here a knife is carried upright on the inside of the weak-side leg. Drawing from this position requires two hands and leaves one's head wide open.

Unless you actually wear your boots outside your pants (or if you're a woman and you habitually wear boots with a skirt or dress) or sit down all day so your hand is within easy reach of your knife, it is tough to draw a knife effectively from a boot carry. To increase your chances of success, arrange the placement of your knife carefully, develop sound tactics to cover your draw, and practice a lot.

Placement of your boot knife boils down to a choice of four basic locations: outside strong-side leg, inside strong-side leg, outside weak-side leg, and inside weak-side leg. For the handle-down carry, the outside of your strong-side leg (meaning the leg corresponding to your strong or preferred weapon hand) or the inside of your weak-side leg are best. With the knife in either of these positions, you can go down

A proper boot knife draw includes guarding the head with the free arm and drawing the knife downward from the outside of the rear leg. Kicks can easily be blocked in this position, clearing the way for a quick counter like the thrust to the groin demonstrated here.

on one knee and guard your head with your free arm (keeping it in front) while you reach under your pant leg and draw your knife. I've had best results with my knife on the outside of my right (strong-side) leg. Assuming a left-side-forward stance, I drop to my right knee and guard my head with my left arm while I reach down and draw my knife with my right hand. This tactic protects my head from kicks and knees and keeps my drawing hand protected from grabs. It also sets up a good opening move in the form of an uppercut thrust to the thigh, groin, or abdomen.

Due to the disadvantages of boot carries, physical tactics alone may not be enough to ensure a successful draw. If you opt for a boot carry, you might want to practice using psychological ploys such as feigning nausea, dropping to one knee, and clutching your stomach when confronted with a threatening situation. This puts your hand close to your knife to make your draw and puts your attacker off guard psychologically.

Boot knives are often described as last ditch weapons. In my opinion, this is only true if you actually do carry them in your boot. Put one in a more accessible place where you can get to it the instant you need it and you've got a formidable weapon that will make even the most determined attacker think twice about his intentions.

SLEEVE CARRIES

Another carry style popular with fictional characters is the sleeve carry, in which the knife sheath is strapped to the inside of the wrist or forearm and concealed beneath a long-sleeve shirt. When danger threatens, our hero reaches into his sleeve, or, more popularly, flicks his wrist, and the knife magically appears in his hand.

As slick as this may seem, it's the movies again. In reality, a knife that is rigged loosely enough to slide into the hand with a flick of the wrist will also slide into the hand (or onto the floor) during many everyday body movements.

Though people have actually carried knives strapped to their forearms, this carry has some serious drawbacks. First of all, the knife is usually strapped to the forearm of the weak hand to allow for a strong-hand draw. Practically, this means you can *only* draw the knife with your strong hand. If your strong hand is injured or disabled, you can't get to your knife with your other hand.

Secondly, unless you habitually wear heavy shirts with snap-fastened or very loose sleeves, you won't be able to conceal a knife effectively in this position or get to it quickly when you need it. The fact that the knife is strapped to your forearm also means that you

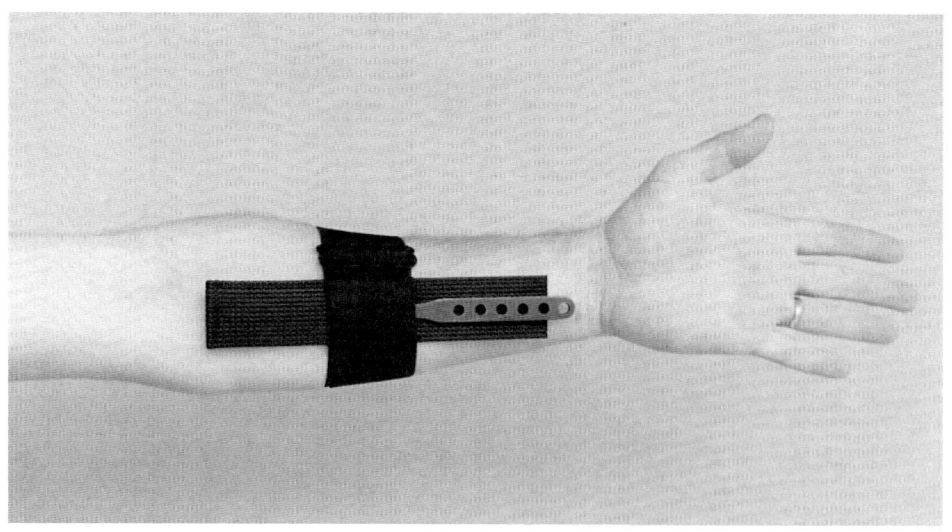

Sleeve knives, such as the Blue Devil from Blackjack, tend to be more mysterious than practical. In addition to being a somewhat uncomfortable carry because of the tapered shape of the forearm, it is likely that the sheath will slide down toward the wrist during a draw. The only sure-fire method of attaching a sleeve knife is with medical adhesive tape, but this will usually cost you some hair.

are restricted to a very flat and relatively short knife.

The greatest disadvantage I've found with sleeve carries, however, is that they typically don't provide for a reliable draw. Because of the tapered shape of the forearm, a sharp tug on the knife handle doesn't normally free the knife, it just moves the whole knife and sheath assembly down around your wrist.

In addition to strapping a sleeve knife to your forearm, it is also possible to sew or Velcro a sheath into the inside of a coat sleeve. This arrangement has all the disadvantages of the forearm carry, as well as forcing you to wear a coat all the time.

I would only consider a sleeve carry in situations where extreme concealment was more important than quick access. I would then carry only a very slim, short knife (probably with a skeletonized handle) in a sheath taped (not strapped) to my forearm with medical tape. Needless to say, this is not a comfortable or handy arrangement for everyday carry.

The best tactic for drawing a sleeve knife, short of secretly slipping it out and having it in your hand before the fight starts, is to stun your opponent with an empty-hand strike or a kick before you go for your blade. If this isn't possible, assume a loose crossed-arm posture with your strong hand on the bottom and your weak hand on top. The strong hand unsnaps the sleeve or slips into the sleeve to find the handle of the knife. Once a firm grip is established, the strong hand pulls back as the weak hand shoots elbow first in the opposite direction. The movement of the weak hand can be transformed easily into an elbow, backhand, or palm heel strike or, even better, an eye gouge. Alternately, the sweep of the free hand can be used to parry or grab, clearing a path for the knife to go in. This may sound easy, but doing it without your opponent seeing it is not. Be prepared for a face full of fist or worse as soon as you start to go for your knife. Better yet, carry your knife somewhere else.

POCKET CARRIES

A fixed blade knife can and has been successfully carried in a pocket. The famed William Ewart Fairbairn, codesigner of the legendary Fairbairn-Sykes fighting knife, regularly carried a boot-knife-sized prototype of this knife in a sheath inserted through a hole cut in the bottom of his front trouser pocket.

Short, lightweight knives with a flat profile can be rigged this way by gluing Velcro (the plastic hook side) around the top of the knife sheath and sewing matching patches of woolly Velcro inside the pocket around the hole. This carry only conceals well when used with relatively baggy pants of reasonably heavy material.

I do not recommend carrying sheath knives in coat pockets or pockets of other articles of clothing which are often taken off and separated from the wearer. Remember, the first rule of knife fighting is to have a knife.

SHOULDER HARNESS CARRY

One carry that has become increasingly popular in recent years is the shoulder harness carry. This uses a shoulder harness, much like that used to support a shoulder holster for a handgun, to carry the knife alongside the ribs under a jacket or shirt. For reasons of safety, concealment, and deployability, knives are usually positioned handle down when carried this way.

When used with a quality harness, this is a very comfortable carry that can be used even with full-sized combat knives. It offers excellent access to the knife with either hand and will still surprise many people who don't expect to see someone pull a knife from that spot. It also works very well when drawing from a seated position or inside a vehicle.

The problems with the shoulder harness carry are that you have to wear a coat or heavy shirt to conceal your rig effectively and, if your knife is found, you'll never convince anyone that you were carrying it for utility purposes.

I should note that some so-called "authorities" have maligned the shoulder harness carry on the grounds that when you go for your knife, your opponent will think you're reaching for a gun and will shoot you. I find this ludicrous. If your opponent does in fact have a gun and you draw a knife, I find it very hard to believe that he would refrain from popping a cap in your ass in the spirit of fair play.

If you're shopping for a shoulder rig, by all means try it on before you buy it. When you try it on, wear the type of coat or shirt you would normally wear and have someone other than the salesman check you out from all angles. Shoulder harnesses often print through light material, leaving an unmistakable outline that announces to the world that you've got something deadly tucked under your arm. A good harness should lie flat and not bunch up.

While you've got the harness on, try moving around to determine how comfortable it is during normal everyday activities. You'll usually find that movements such as reaching forward with both hands simultaneously are the least comfortable and that your movement may actually be restricted somewhat. While you're moving around, also check to see if the harness or the position of the knife shifts appreciably. The harness should move with you, yet return to a relaxed position when you do.

One often overlooked consideration when choosing a shoulder harness is color. Obviously, the closer the harness is to the color of the shirts you usually wear, the less likely it will be noticed if your coat flies open unexpectedly. Despite this fact, many makers still offer their harnesses only in basic black. That's great if you wear black shirts all the time, but if you don't, consider having a custom rig made to match the color of your favorite shirts.

A number of shoulder harnesses designed specifically for knives are commercially available. One of the first widely available shoulder rigs was sold with an optional package that was available for the Gerber Guardian boot knife. This package included a Velcro-backed sheath, a leather panel with a matching Velcro patch, and an adjustable elastic harness. This kit also included an elastic and Velcro forearm/ankle harness and was one of the first commercial attempts to offer a personal defense knife with accessories that would allow for a variety of styles of carry.

Although the Guardian system was an ambitious effort, it didn't work nearly as well in practice as it did on paper. The elastic shoulder harness was tight and restrictive. To mount the knife to the harness, the harness had to be passed through one of the belt slots in the leather panel and the Velcro sheath attached to the panel. When this was all done and you finally got your arms slipped through the harness (a major feat not easily accomplished alone), the elastic would pull the leather uncomfortably into your armpit, cutting off the circulation to that arm.

The good thing about the Guardian system was that the elastic harness lay very flat against the body and could be worn under a shirt without any telltale harness lines showing through. Because of the aforementioned drawbacks, however, it usually could not be worn for very long. The Guardian boot knife has since been redesigned by Gerber and, to the best of my knowledge, the concealment option package is no longer available.

One of the more practical and low-profile shoulder harness systems available today is the brainchild of noted cutlery designer Blackie Collins. It is available through Cutlery Shoppe of Boise, Idaho, and is designed to be mated with the excellent custom Kydex sheaths produced by Cutlery Shoppe's Sheath Tech department. The craftsmen of this department can turn out custom speed break Kydex sheaths for practically any design of knife and offer sheath styles with inside-the-pants, boot clip, belt loop, or Bianchi-style military pistol belt attachments in addition to sheaths compatible with this shoulder harness. Workmanship is strictly first class, and prices are very affordable.

Unlike most shoulder rigs, which use some form of figure eight harness, the Blackie Collins design uses an elongated single loop of nylon webbing with a short section of elastic and a suspender-style clip attached to the end. The loop fits over the strong arm, while the remainder of the harness passes behind the neck, in front of the weak-side shoulder, and is secured with the clip to the waistband on the weak side. The knife sheath is attached upside down to the vertical portion of the webbing on the weak side via a nylon buckle and a loop of elastic.

This is a very simple but effective design that is adaptable to many styles of knives. Thanks to the elastic between the harness and the waistband clip, the harness remains very comfortable during movement. The knife is positioned well for a speedy draw with either hand, yet conceals better than some more

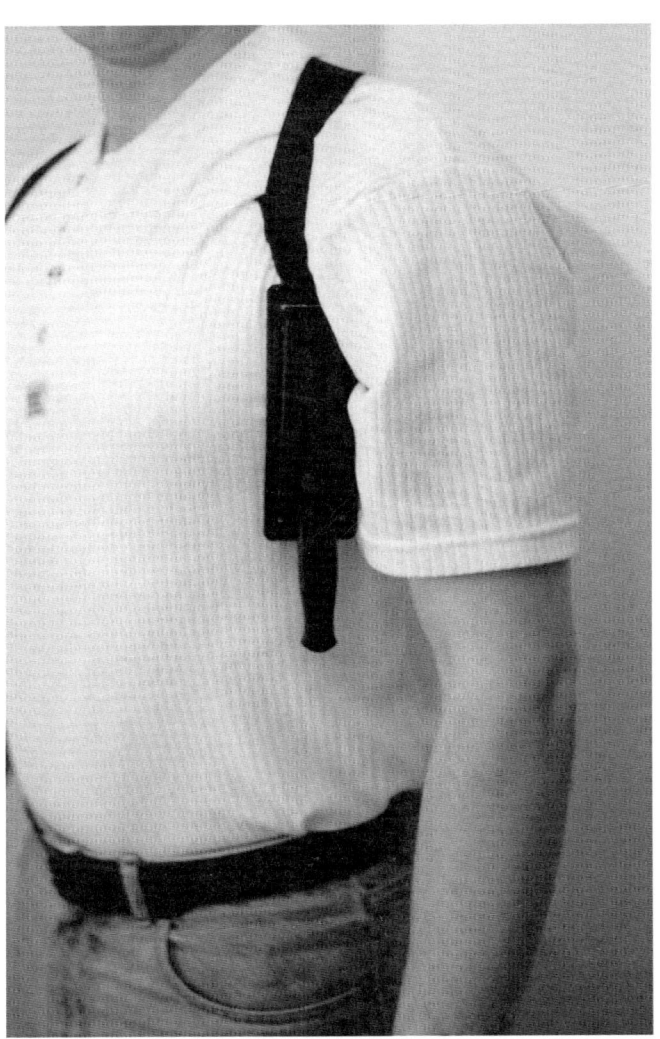
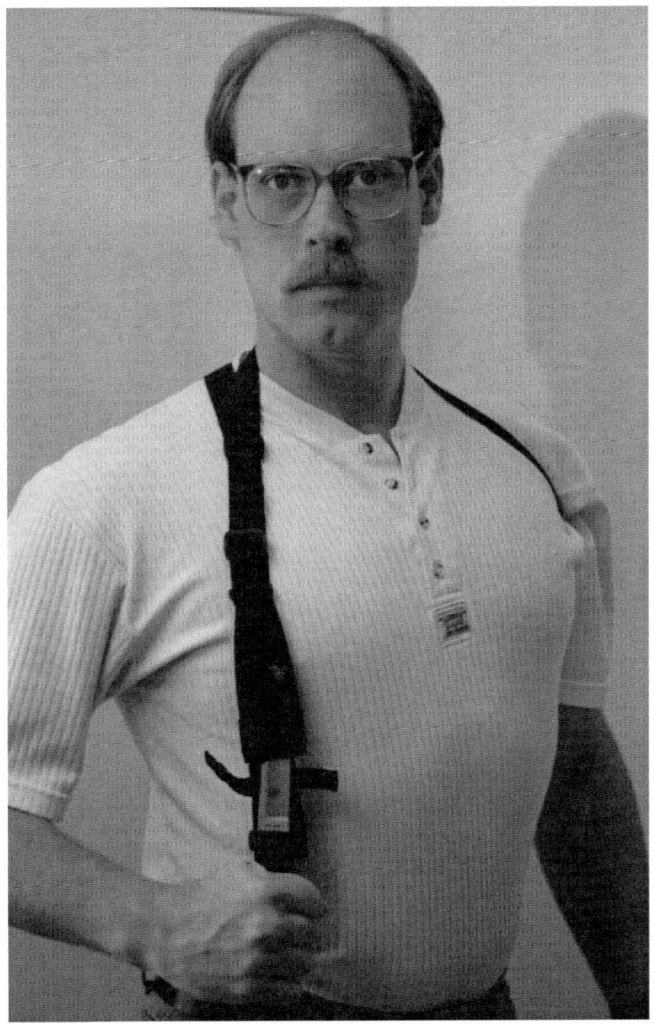

The Blackie Collins shoulder rig sold by Cutlery Shoppe consists of only one shoulder loop and a tie-down strap that secures to the belt or waistband. The only drawback of this simple and effective system is that the harness strap behind the neck tends to ride up and become visible. For good concealment, it should be worn only with collared shirts.

Custom knife maker James S. Piorek, aka Blade Rigger, makes the best shoulder rigs available today. His Execulite™ model (shown here with a genuine rayskin laminated Kydex sheath and Aquatic Fighter™ double edged fighting knife) features an optional anchor strap at the back, which keeps the harness very flat and concealable while allowing it to move with the body.

traditional rigs because the design means that less harness material is exposed to view. My only criticism of the design is that, because the end of the harness loop passes behind the neck and over the opposite shoulder, it sometimes rides up on the neck where it could become visible. This problem usually only occurs when wearing shirts without collars. Collared shirts conceal the harness below the collar and offer much better concealment.

The best knife shoulder rigs I have come across are those offered by James S. Piorek. His Execulite™ system not only incorporates strategically placed sections of elastic into the nylon harness to allow it to expand and flex with the wearer, it includes a special adjustable elastic tie-down strap that runs from the "X" at the center of the harness vertically down to the waistband. This removable strap, along with the well-

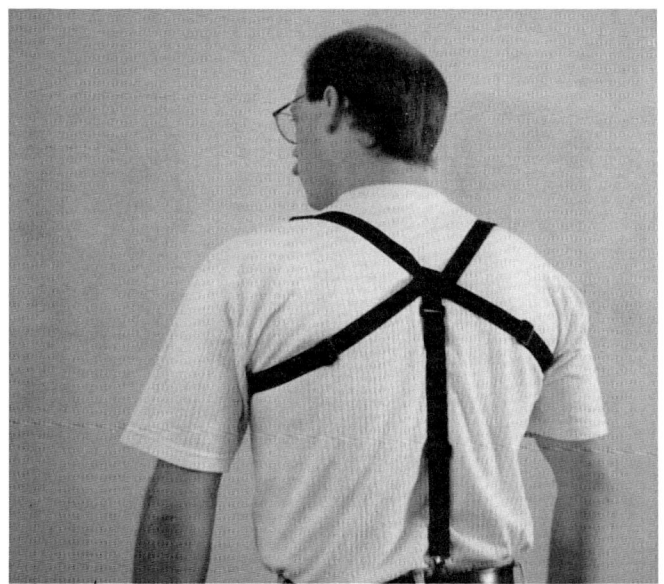

conceived design of the harness, allows the harness to fit and move with the wearer better than any other design I've tried. The strap also keeps the harness flat, maximizing concealment even under very light jackets and windbreakers. In fact, this harness system can actually be worn comfortably and fully concealed on bare skin under a T-shirt.

Another feature of Piorek's Execulite™ design worthy of note is the exclusive combination of elastic sections and sheath pivot points, which allow the sheath to pivot

A jacket is not necessary to effectively conceal a shoulder harness. Here a harness is worn under a snap-fastened shirt. Drawing is accomplished by first opening the shirt Superman style, then pulling the blade. This carry works best under a loose-fitting opaque shirt. Button-fastened shirts can be converted by sewing buttons to the top layer of the shirt and putting snap fasteners underneath.

when the knife is grasped for a draw. This feature allows the user to draw the knife safely in practically any direction, even out of a partially zippered coat or jacket. This is unlike other designs that limit draws to a straight down path. Piorek's shoulder rig weighs a scant five ounces and is extremely comfortable to wear.

In most cases, a shoulder harness will have to be worn under a jacket or sweater, which, ideally, should be worn unzipped or partially zipped to conceal the rig and the knife handle, yet allow for a quick draw. Sometimes, however, cold or inclement weather will require that you wear your jacket closed. Although it is possible to reach under short jackets to draw your knife, this causes the clearing path of the blade to come awfully close to your own body, and you can easily cut yourself. A better solution is to purchase a jacket with a snap-fastened flap over the zipper. When you need to wear the jacket closed, snap the flap shut but don't use the zipper. When danger threatens you can pull the flap and pop the snaps with your free hand and go for a normal draw with your strong hand. In many cases this can be accomplished almost as quickly as a draw that begins with an open jacket.

In warm weather, wearing any type of jacket to conceal a shoulder rig can be either very uncomfortable or a dead giveaway that you're carrying. One way to overcome this drawback is to wear your rig under a shirt with snap fasteners or a loose pullover shirt worn outside your pants. With the former, drawing your knife is accomplished by first pulling your shirt open à la Superman, then reaching for your knife. With the latter, you simply reach under your shirt and grab your knife. With practice, these methods can be extremely fast and offer an amazing variety of dress possibilities with a single carry. To play it safe, choose baggy shirts made from sturdy, opaque material and get a harness that either matches your undershirt color or your flesh tone.

By the way, if you like the idea of the "Superman"-style carry under a shirt but have a closet full of button-down shirts, all is not lost. Just remove the buttons from your shirt and replace them with snaps. Then sew the buttons in place over the existing button holes to retain the shirt's original style.

Deployment of a knife from a shoulder harness normally begins with clearing the jacket or shirt with the free hand to allow the strong hand to reach in and retrieve the knife. With a jacket, the weak hand grasps the zipper area on the side where the knife is carried and pulls the jacket away from the body and slightly out from the body's centerline. Don't exaggerate this movement or move your weak hand too far from the centerline because it leaves you exposed and makes it difficult to get your weak hand back into action to check, strike, or defend against an incoming attack.

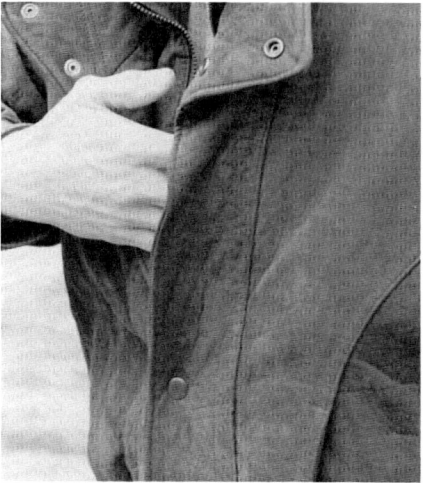

Here knife maker James S. Piorek demonstrates a draw from one of his custom shoulder rigs. Piorek's harnesses include strategically placed elastic panels and pivot points that allow the knife to be drawn at a wide variety of angles, such as the high-angle draw from a partially zipped jacket demonstrated here.

The strong hand then moves under the jacket, firmly grasps as much of the exposed handle as possible, unsnaps any retaining straps present, and executes the draw. To avoid having your knife arm "jammed" or immobilized by your opponent's pressing it against your body, keep your strong side away from your opponent throughout the draw and execute the draw in a downward arc, extending your arm by straightening the elbow.

As you execute the draw, you can continue the natural motion of your free hand clearing your jacket for the draw and execute a palm heel strike or eye jab. These strikes can either be real or feints to create an opening to go in with your knife. You can also use your weak hand to sweep your opponent's hands aside or to grab his clothing or hair before you put your blade to work.

If your strong hand is injured or immobilized, you can easily execute a weak-hand draw from a shoulder harness carry by sweeping your jacket aside with the extended thumb of your weak hand, grasping the knife handle firmly, releasing any retaining straps, and executing the draw. The drawing line of the knife will follow a downward and slightly forward arc.

Drawing from a shoulder rig worn under a snap-fastened shirt is basically the same as with a jacket, except that the draw must be preceded by the Superman move described earlier. If you wear your rig with button-down or pullover shirts, the shirts must be worn outside your pants. The weak hand lifts the shirt up and away from the body so the strong hand can reach under and pull straight down to draw.

Weak-hand drawing from under button-down or pullover shirts is best accomplished by pulling the shirt up to expose the handle of the knife and then drawing. Snaking the hand under the shirt to set up a draw is too slow, and it is likely that the knife will snag on the inside of the shirt as it is withdrawn.

One alternative to the shoulder harness that provides for a similar style of carry is pinning or clipping your knife upside down to the lining of your jacket. Improvised carries of this type can be as fast on the draw as a conventional shoulder harness carry but tend not to hold the knife as reliably.

The slickest adaptation of this type of carry I've seen is

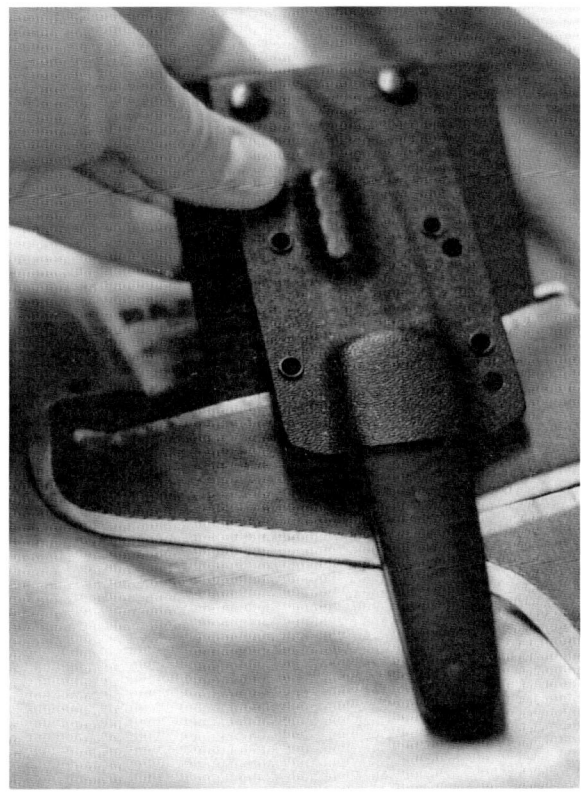

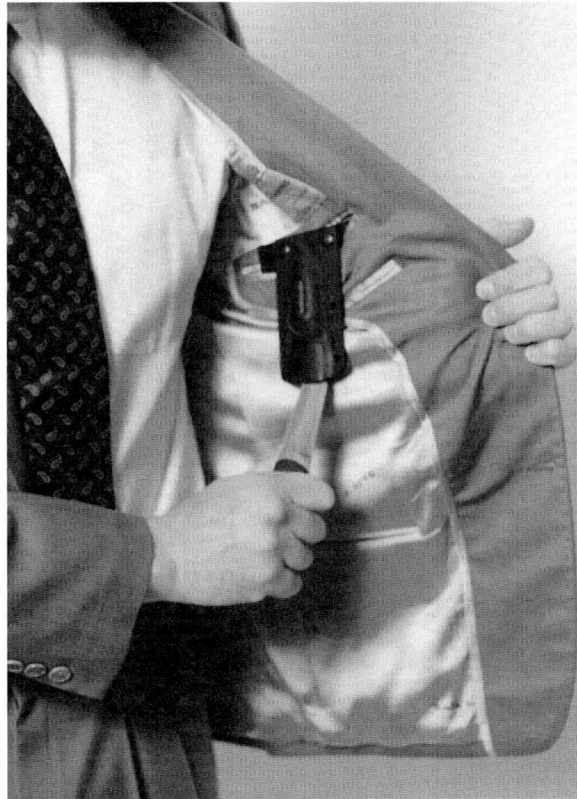

For suit-and-tie types, there is no better choice than Bud Nealy's MCS in the breast pocket carry mode. The sheath is fitted with the large Kydex panel included with the kit and simply inserted into the breast pocket. The flat profile and light weight of the design make it very unobtrusive. Best of all, in a secure environment, the jacket and knife can be removed in full view of anyone without alerting him to the presence of the knife. With a traditional shoulder harness carry this would be impossible.

When faced with a possible threat, assume a crossed-armed posture while slipping your hand into your jacket to grasp your knife. Your free hand and arm should be over your strong hand. From here you can parry or strike with your free hand as you draw your blade.

the breast pocket carry mode offered with Bud Nealy's MCS sheath system. For this carry, a wide, flat panel of Kydex supplied with the system is attached with Chicago-style bolts to the base of the knife's Kydex sheath. The knife and sheath are then inverted and the Kydex panel slipped securely into the interior breast pocket of a suit coat, blazer, jacket, or vest. The knife is therefore suspended upside down in a perfect position for a quick draw. Since Bud Nealy designs his knives so they are exceptionally slim and lightweight, there is no telltale bulge or shifting of the jacket to reveal the knife's presence.

This carry is probably the best choice for executives and others who habitually wear suits. Unlike a shoulder harness, this system allows the wearer to remove his jacket and knife without attracting attention when in a secure environment. Removing a suit jacket to expose a shoulder rig will no doubt raise some eyebrows at the office.

This version of Nealy's MCS carry system can also be an ideal choice for women. Rather than placing the Kydex panel into a breast pocket, a woman can slip it over the side panel of her bra so it rides comfortably under her arm. In this position, the knife handle rides high enough to still be comfortable while sitting, yet low enough to be accessible by reaching under a pullover shirt or sweater. It can also be worn under a snap-fastened shirt for a "Superwoman"-style draw. This draw, when used by a woman, would have the added advantage that the sudden opening of her blouse could shock her attacker and buy an extra second to either get in a disabling cut or thrust or make a hasty exit. If a woman is faced with a sexual assault, it could also be used as a ruse in which she feigns compliance to allow her to draw her blade. Because the sheath must remain anchored to allow for a reliable draw, this carry works best with sports-style bras.

If you opt for any variation of the shoulder harness carry and find yourself in a situation which may require that you draw your weapon, you can assume a defensive posture from which you can draw your blade instantly. At the first sign of trouble, assume a balanced standing posture with your strong side to the rear. Cross your arms by placing your strong hand casually inside your jacket on the handle of your knife while concealing this movement by crossing your other arm in front so it ends up cupping your strong-side elbow. From this position, you are poised to strike or defend with your weak hand while simultaneously drawing your knife with your strong hand. Practice crossing your arms in this manner frequently until the movement becomes natural.

NECK CORD CARRY

The neck cord carry is one of the few carry methods that is compatible with almost any style of dress. It is an ideal choice for joggers, bikers, and others who often venture out in public clad only in shorts and a T-shirt. As its name implies, this carry is accomplished by hanging your knife and sheath on a cord around

The neck carry is a convenient and comfortable method of carrying lightweight knives. The cord should be adjusted so the butt of the knife rides just above the navel. This way the knife will not bulge away from the body when you sit down. This carry is demonstrated here with a Nealy Aikuchi and MCS sheath.

your neck. Typically, the cord is attached to the bottom of the sheath so the knife hangs inverted and can be released with a firm tug.

Although very small knives could conceivably be carried on a neck cord in open view, most knives large enough to be used for personal defense should be carried under a shirt or jacket. This carry works best with pullover shirts and sweaters that are worn outside the pants, allowing the hand to reach up under the shirt to execute the draw. Do *not* try to draw your knife by pulling the cord up like you're getting a bucket of water from a well. This is far too slow to be effective and will probably result in your being strangled with your own sheath cord before you ever get your knife out.

This carry can also be used with button-down shirts in the Superman style, but you'll find that your knife can often be spotted through the gaps between the shirt snaps.

Neck cord carries generally work best when your knife is covered by only one layer of clothing at any particular time. For example, if you're using a Superman carry and decide to put on a sweater or jacket that is closed in front, move your knife from under your shirt and place it between your shirt and the outer garment. This way, you won't have to undress completely before you can get to your knife.

One of the most difficult things to determine when wearing a knife on a neck cord is how long the cord should be to balance deployability, concealment, and comfort. A good rule of thumb is to hang your knife so the butt of the handle is even with the top of your navel when you are standing erect. For most people of average build, the knife will lie reasonably flat and the tip of the sheath will fall in the hollow of the sternum. When you sit, the knife handle will drop slightly but will remain just above the belt line. When worn in this way, most small knives will not swing out excessively when you bend forward, revealing their presence.

Many types of cord can be used to rig a neck carry, but the primary considerations when choosing a cord are strength, comfort, and low profile. Above all, the cord must be strong enough not to break when the knife is drawn. It should also be thick enough so as not to cut into the neck during carry or the stress of a draw. Finally, the style of the cord should not attract undue attention.

My favorite choice for neck carry cord is military parachute cord or "550 cord." This cord consists of an inner core made up of multiple strands of braided nylon covered by an outer nylon sheath. It comes in various colors and has a breaking strength of 550 pounds (hence the name "550 cord"). It is thick enough to support the weight of a knife comfortably and does not attract much attention. 550 cord is available through most military surplus dealers.

Other cords that work well include leather thongs, shoelaces, and thin mountaineering utility cords. Although it is possible to use a decorative metal chain as a platform for a neck carry, most chains are too weak to stand up to the stress of a quick draw.

The most refined neck carry systems I've seen are offered by James S. Piorek. His neck carry sheaths incorporate features such as adjustable cord fittings (Cord Jam(TM)) to vary the length of the cord and a unique elastic retaining strap that fits around the wearer's chest to keep the knife close to the body even when bending forward. This design features a quick release and allows for movement and body expansion during breathing.

Bud Nealy's well-conceived MCS sheaths also come predrilled for attachment of a neck cord. The light weight and flat profile of both Nealy's knives and sheaths make them extremely comfortable and concealable when used with a neck cord carry. I regularly carry my Nealy *Aikuchi* on a neck cord under a polo shirt or sometimes even a T-shirt. Even my wife, who knows how and where I like to carry my knives, often doesn't realize I'm carrying it.

I have a great fondness for balisong knives and recently designed a custom Kydex scabbard for a latchless balisong that allows it to be carried on a neck cord. Built to my specifications by the Sheath Tech department of Cutlery Shoppe, this rig holds my closed knife securely in place in the inverted position. A quick pull on the knife frees it from the sheath positioned in my hand for an instant opening.

A variation of the neck carry that can be utilized by women again uses a brassiere as a carry platform. With this method, a knife is hung upside down from the front center of the

James S. Piorek's custom neck carry rig features a strap that keeps the knife and sheath from swinging out away from the torso. The Custom Kwaiken knife shown here is also curved to conform to the body contour for better concealment.

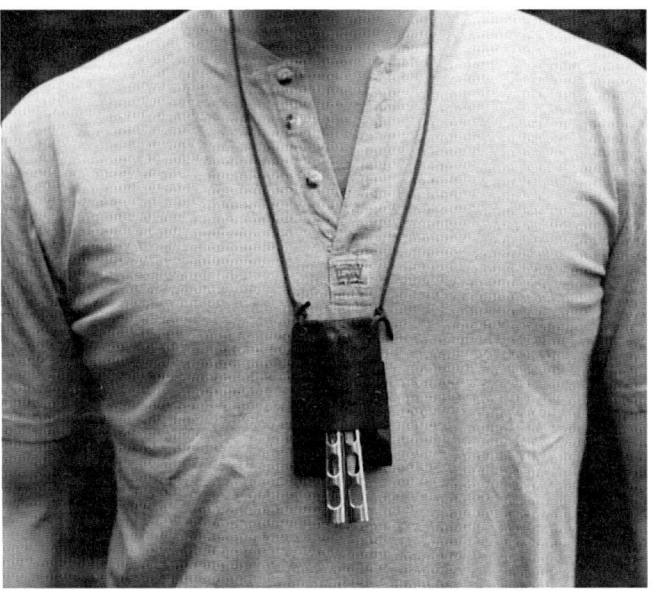

Sheath-Tech, a division of Cutlery Shoppe of Boise, ID, offers an excellent line of Kydex sheaths for both production and custom knives. This sheath was custom crafted to the author's design to hold a latchless balisong. Shown here in a neck cord carry position, it also features an integral belt loop for belt carry.

bra, placing it in the same position as a typical neck carry while obviating the need for a neck cord. Sheaths that feature inverted boot clips, such as the current production Gerber Guardian and the Nealy MCS package, are natural choices for this carry.

OBJECT CARRIES

A final method of carrying a fixed blade knife is to attach it to or place it in an object that is carried in the hand. When done properly, this carry method can allow you to literally have your knife in hand without anyone knowing it. Obviously, this is a tremendous advantage if you are attacked.

Before we discuss specific object carries, let me make it clear that this mode of carry does not mean dropping a knife into your briefcase or purse and hitting the streets. If you are attacked, it is extremely likely that you will be quickly separated from these items and almost a certainty that you will not have the luxury of digging through their contents to retrieve your knife. Basically, if you can't have your hand on your knife in less than two seconds, you can't count on being able to use it in a fight.

The number and type of object carries possible are limited only by your imagination. I'll describe some of the ones I have used here, but you need to examine your habits and environment to develop carries that work best for you.

The paper bag carry is one of the most basic and effective object carries. With this carry, an unsheathed straight blade knife is held in a standard grip in the hand. To conceal it from view, a small paper bag is placed over the knife and held in place by the thumb or the thumb and forefinger. In this way, you can literally walk around in public with your knife poised and ready to go in an instant. If you're attacked, you can either release the grip on the bag and let it fall away to reveal your knife or, better yet, wait for your attacker to get close enough and thrust right through the bag into him.

A similar type of object carry can be accomplished by placing your unsheathed knife in an envelope. If necessary, the envelope can actually be sealed and the handle of the knife grasped from the outside of the envelope. When brought into action, the knife will easily penetrate the envelope and your hapless attacker. Make sure you remember which end of the envelope contains the handle of the knife so you don't inadvertently grab the blade (use the stamp as a marker).

Obviously, this tactic is adaptable to any type of object that can effectively conceal a knife and afford a modicum of protection against the sharp blade and point, yet be easily punctured if you choose to thrust through it. Other objects that would lend themselves to this kind of carry would include newspapers, magazines, handkerchiefs, shirts, jackets, plastic bags, and hats. In cold weather, this technique can be used with gloves and mittens as well. One particularly effective

Carry Options for Fixed Blade Knives

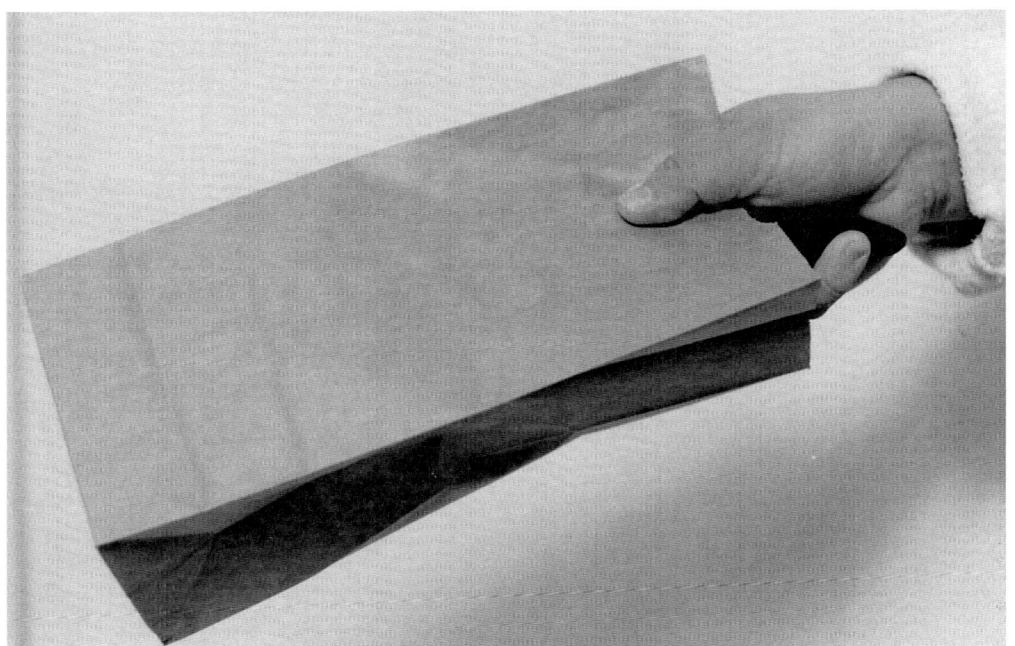

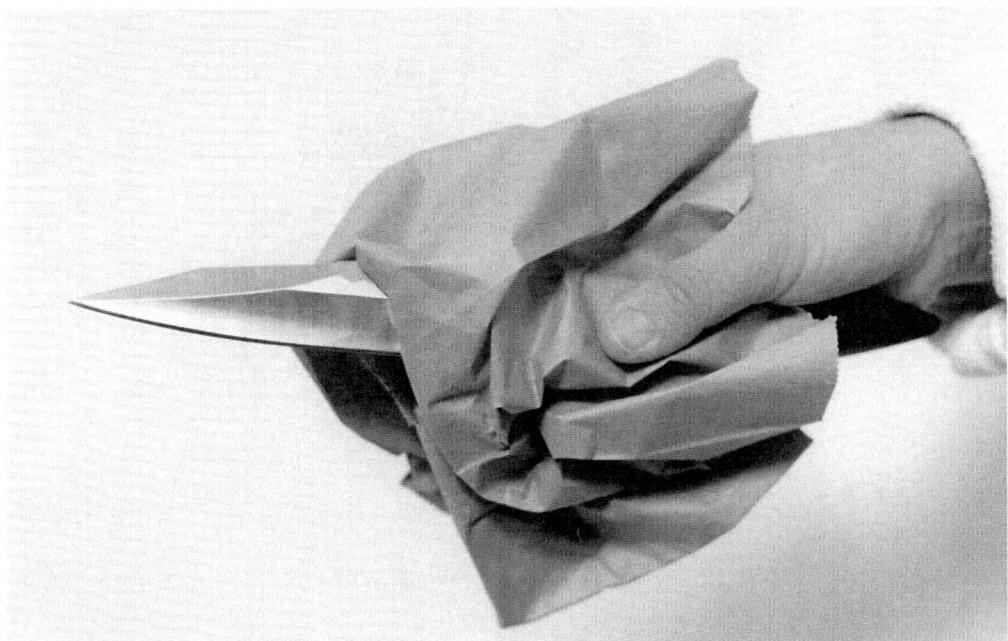

An excellent carry method when danger is imminent is to hold a knife ready in your hand while concealing it from view with a paper bag. Done properly, it offers a very benign appearance. In the event of trouble, a good surprise move is to thrust right through the bag into your attacker.

method is to conceal a push dirk (a small knife that has its handle affixed perpendicularly to the blade to form a "T") in your closed hand inside a glove. When needed, you can either thrust directly through the glove or pull the glove off with your free hand or teeth to expose the blade.

I generally feel that defensive knives should be carried on your person rather than attached to an object that could easily be dropped or grabbed during an attack. However, there is no rule that prevents you from carrying a quick deployment knife attached to or mounted within a commonly carried object *in addition to* your primary carry knife. Since the object being carried is already in the hand,

For trips to the ATM, there is no better companion than James S. Piorek's CKB-Alpha.™ This stylish and fully functional checkbook cover conceals a wickedly sharp blade, which is drawn with the assistance of a short lanyard. The beauty of this design is that the blade can actually be drawn as you surrender your checkbook by retaining your grip on the knife's lanyard as the checkbook is pulled away.

such a knife could be instantly available to deliver an initial cut or thrust in response to an attack. Often this is all that is needed to put an end to an encounter. If your attacker persists, you can use the time you bought with your initial strike to draw your main defensive knife and use it instead of, or in conjunction with, your first blade.

One very innovative example of this strategy is the CKB-Alpha™ made by custom knifemaker James S. Piorek. This design conceals an all-steel, tanto-style knife within a fully functional leather checkbook cover. The knife is actually stored completely concealed within a Kydex sheath that is built into the checkbook cover. The slim profile of both knife and sheath adds no bulk and maintains the appearance of a standard checkbook. Attached to the butt end of the knife is a braided lanyard which extends out of the cover. Grasp the lanyard with the little and ring fingers of the hand and give a tug, and the knife slides out of the checkbook and directly into a firm fighting grip. The design

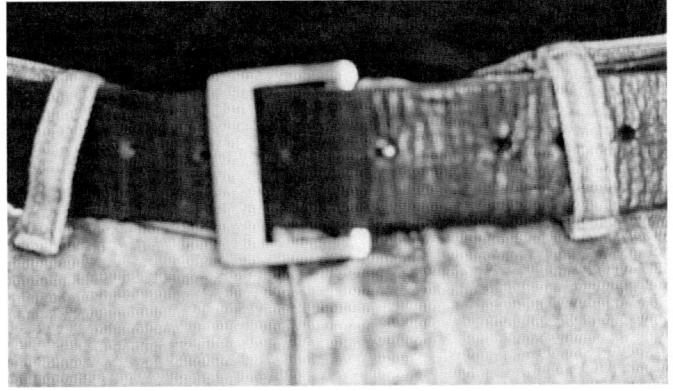

Belt buckle knives are interesting collector's pieces but are not practical for personal defense. In addition to being uncomfortable in the hand, when drawn, most cease to hold up your pants.

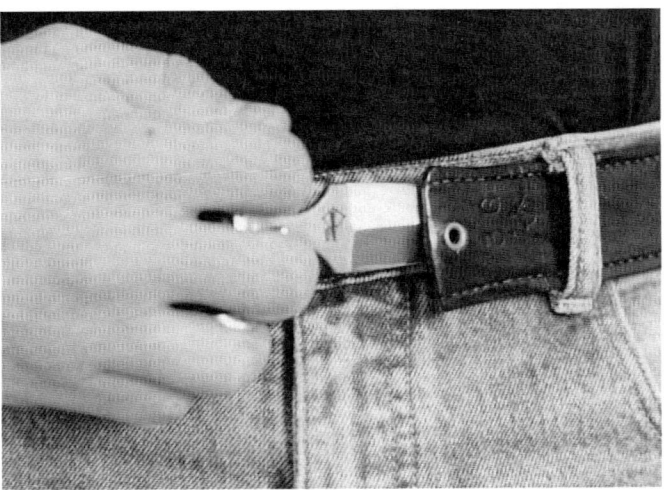
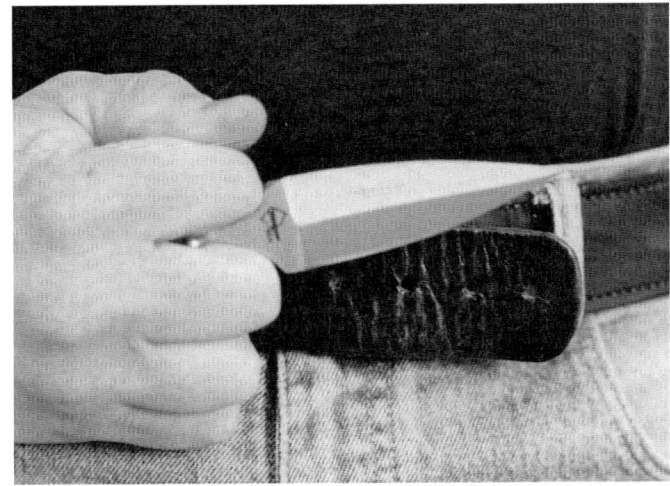

of the knife includes a tapered butt and a cutout hole for a thumb purchase. Together, these features allow a very secure grip on this knife, which may be the ideal companion for your next trip to the ATM.

A number of knife companies, most notably Cold Steel, offer knives with sheaths that have an attached key ring. These small knives can indeed serve as key rings and are instantly deployable when you carry your keys in your hand (as you should when approaching your home or car). Again, such knives are not intended as primary defensive tools. As an opening move to buy time to run or access a more formidable weapon, however, they are a useful item to add to your arsenal.

Two other types of object carry that deserve mention are the wallet knife and the belt buckle knife. Wallet knives typically consist of small, all-steel push dirk knives that fit into your existing wallet or, more commonly, a specially designed leather wallet. The idea with these knives is that, when faced with a mugging situation, you make a natural move for your wallet and come out instead with a sharp piece of steel. While I agree completely with the idea of carrying a knife where your wallet is supposed to be, I'd much rather have that knife be a substantial folding knife or boot knife than a tiny push dirk.

Belt buckle knives, as their name implies, are knives designed to look like and function as belt buckles. The most famous of these is the Bowen Belt Knife, a stout stainless-steel push dirk available in both single and double-edged formats. The blade of this knife fits into a sheath built into a specially designed belt. The handle of the knife acts as the belt buckle, and a pin which protrudes through the front face of the knife fits through holes in each end of the belt to hold the belt securely to the wearer.

The biggest problem with this design is that as soon as the knife is drawn, the belt no longer functions as a belt. To most people this doesn't matter too much, but others might find themselves assuming a fighting stance with one hand on their blade and the other holding up their sagging drawers. For such people, a backup pair of suspenders is probably the best solution. Some custom makers have designed rigs that continue to function as belts even after the knife is drawn. However, all belt buckle designs require that the knife be curved to follow the contour of the wearer's body. This usually gives these knives a somewhat uncomfortable feel in the hand and makes precision slashes and thrusts very difficult to perform. My advice is to use your belt to hold your pants up and find another place to carry your knife.

CHAPTER 4

Opening Folding Knives One-Handed

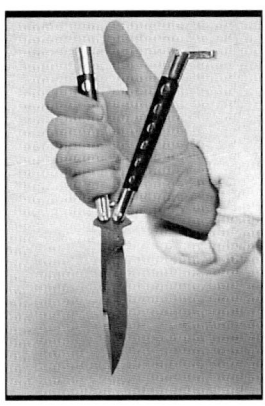

As explained earlier, one of the disadvantages of a folding knife for personal defense is that it takes two distinct actions to bring the knife into play: it must first be retrieved from its carry position, then it must be opened. With practice, however, most designs of folding knives can be opened swiftly with only one hand. Mastery of one-handed openings not only expedites the deployment of the knife, it also allows you to bring your knife into play when your other hand is injured, holding an auxiliary weapon or shield, or otherwise occupied.

A word of warning before I discuss specific opening methods: one-handed openings require dexterity and large amounts of practice to do correctly. When you first begin learning these methods, it is very likely that you will drop your knife or contact the blade edge with your hand and fingers. For this reason, I highly recommend that you purchase a second knife identical to your carry knife and dull the edge and round the point on a grinder or with a file. Use this practice knife to learn and practice the opening techniques. Do not try any technique with a sharp knife until you've perfected it using a dulled practice knife. The dulled practice knife is also the ideal tool for safely practicing drawing your defensive folder from concealment quickly.

It makes sense that a knife that has been

The best way to learn one-handed opening techniques and practice high-speed draws safely is to buy two identical knives and dull the edge of one with a file or grinder. Perfect all your blade-handling skills with this knife before moving on to a sharp blade.

"broken in" and operates smoothly will be easier to open one-handed. To make the action of your lockback folding knife slicker, put a pinch of automobile buffing compound or jeweler's rouge and a little oil in the joint of your knife and work the blade back and forth a few hundred times. This will polish the mating surfaces of the blade and locking bar. Then, thoroughly rinse the polishing compound out with water or alcohol and lubricate the joint with WD-40 or a Teflon-bearing gun lubricant. For liner lock knives, regular cleaning and good lubrication are all that's needed to keep them opening smoothly.

Since lockback folding knives are the most commonly carried folding knives, we will look at one-handed openings for them first. Several factors determine the ease with which a lockback folder can be opened. The most important of these is the amount of the blade that remains exposed when the knife is in the closed position. Knives that almost totally conceal the blade when closed are very difficult to open one-handed, since there is very little area to grip or gain purchase with the thumb.

The length of the locking bar and stiffness of its spring also affect the ease with which a knife can be opened. Generally, so-called "center lock" or "forward lock" knives that have locking bars approximately half the length of the knife handle are easiest to open.

Finally, the weight of the blade in relation to the handle determines whether the blade can be opened by using gravity or inertial opening techniques. The heavier the blade is in relation to the handle, the easier these techniques are to perform.

Note that all of the openings described for lockback folders work well, if not better, with liner lock folders. Liner lock knives generally exert very little pressure on the blade to keep it in the closed position and therefore tend to open more smoothly and with less effort than lockback knives.

THUMB OPENINGS

The most basic type of one-handed opening for a folding knife is the thumb opening. To perform this opening, grip the closed knife by placing it blade up in the crease at the base of your four fingers. Curl your fingers tightly around the handle to anchor it into that crease. Now place the ball of your thumb on the nail nick of the blade and push straight out. As the blade begins to

Opening Folding Knives One-Handed

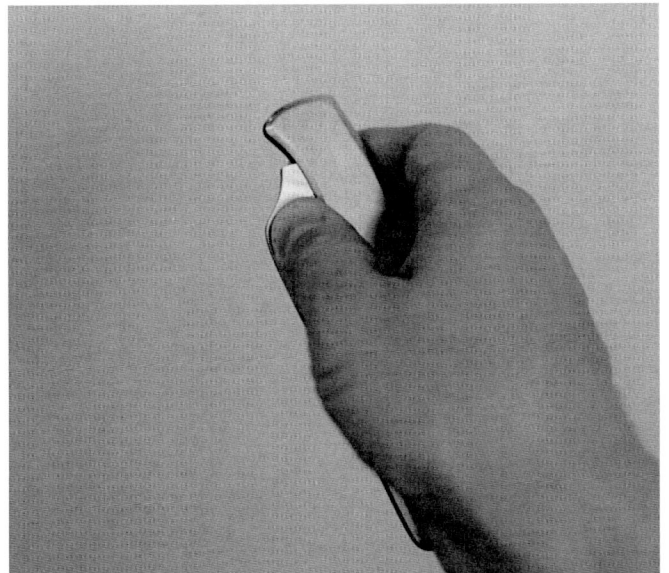

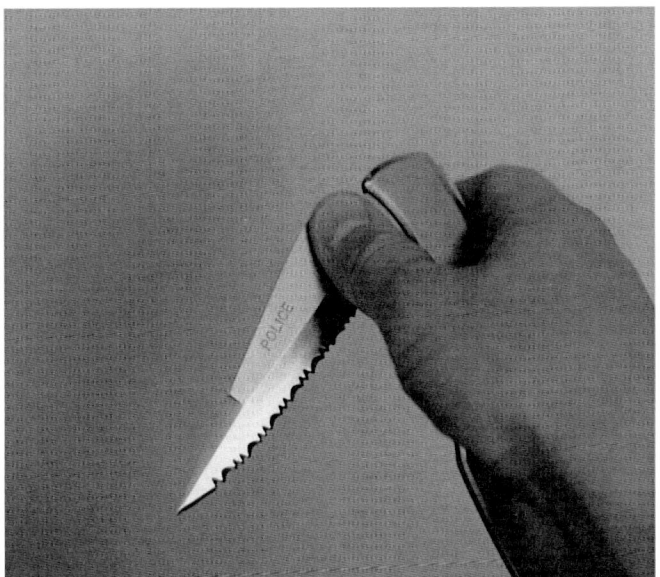

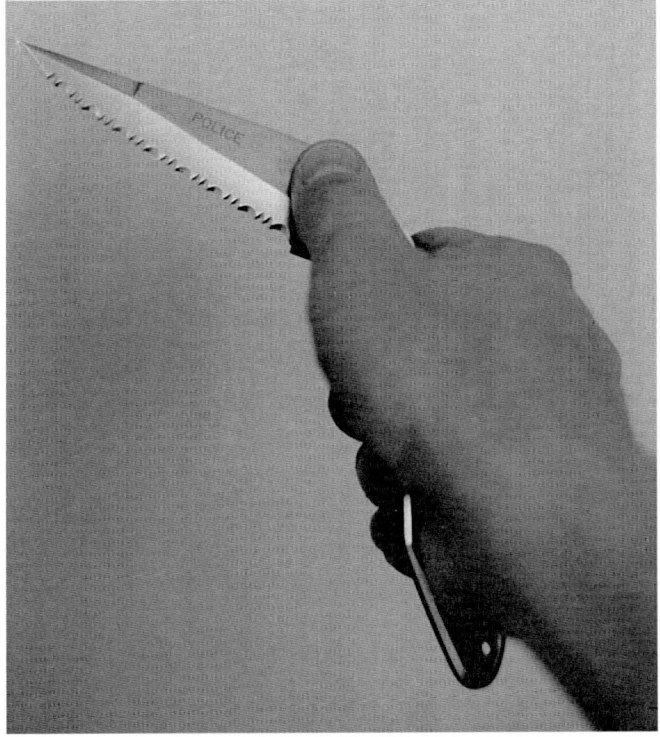

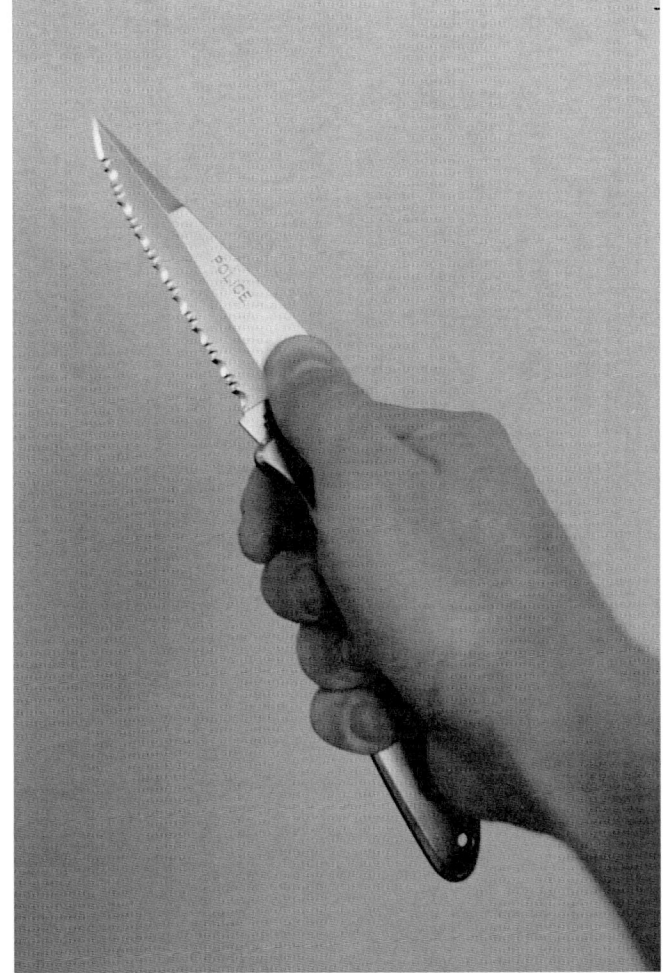

The thumb-opening method of opening a folding knife one-handed. Although this can be done with any folder that has enough blade surface exposed in the closed position to offer a purchase for the thumb, it works best with knives that have a built-in thumb purchase on the blade. It is demonstrated here with a Spyderco Police Model.

open, push in a circular arc with your thumb to rotate the blade into the open position. For very stiff knives, you can use your index or middle finger to help start the opening by pinching the blade between that finger and your thumb.

Instead of rotating the blade all the way open, you can also start the opening with your fingers and finish it by flicking your wrist. Once the blade is open about 30 degrees, flick your wrist quickly and the inertia of the blade will complete the opening. Gerber folding knives are best suited for this type of opening because their blades have a special intermediate safety notch cut into the surface of the tang that contacts the locking bar. This is designed to stop the blade about 60 degrees from the closed position during closing to prevent it from snapping shut on your fingers. It works equally well when opening the knife. When the blade is thumbed open about 45 degrees, it slips into this safety notch. From there it is easily flicked open.

One old trick used by street knife fighters was to wedge a wooden matchstick into the handle slot of a folding knife to keep the blade from closing completely. This made thumbing the knife open much easier, but it also exposed the knife point, making it likely that you'd stab yourself in the hand if you reached into your pocket quickly. For this reason, I do not recommend this practice.

About 20 years ago, a company designed a small attachment for folding knives which allowed them to be opened very quickly with one hand. This device, shaped from nickel-plated spring steel, was called a *Flicket*. It was installed by drifting it onto the back of the blade with a screwdriver until it was positioned near the hinge pin. The raised lever of the Flicket offered an excellent thumb purchase and great leverage, allowing the knife to be thumbed open with the speed of a good switchblade. I carried a Flicket-equipped Gerber Folding Sportsman II for about 10 years and was very pleased with the way it performed. The only drawbacks of the Flicket design were that it tended to wear through pockets rather quickly, it prevented the knife from being used with some belt sheaths, and it was not ambidextrous.

To my knowledge, Flickets are no longer made. However, a similar device called the *One Armed Bandit* is available and offers the same thumb purchase of the Flicket. This device is barrel-shaped and secures to the knife blade with a set screw. It offers a slimmer profile than the Flicket and is ambidextrous. It does not, however, offer the same leverage as a Flicket and is therefore a bit slower.

In recent years, the idea of adding a thumb purchase to the blade of a folding knife has become very popular with commercial knife manufacturers and custom cutlers. Many knife companies offer folders with thumb studs or thumb bobs attached to one or both sides of their blades. In most cases, these attachments work reasonably well. Some,

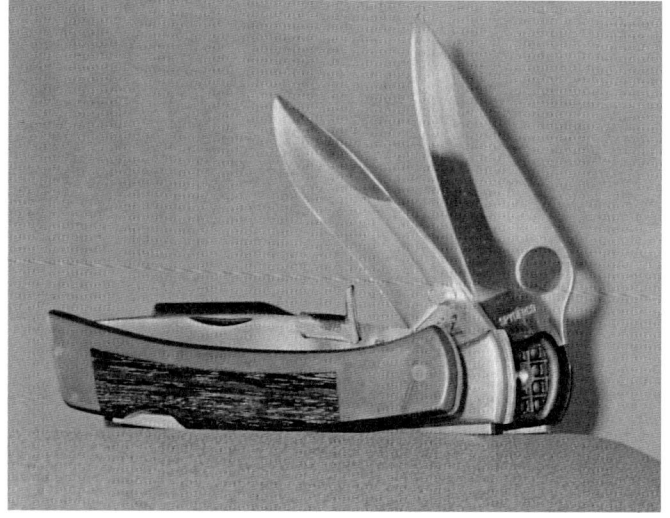

Many recent folding knife designs include thumb purchases to allow them to be opened quickly with one hand. Shown here are the author's Gerber Folding Sportsman II with a Flicket opening attachment, a Blackjack Knives Folding Mamba with an ambidextrous opening stud, and a Spyderco Endura with its patented opening hole. Of all the designs the author has tried, the Spyderco hole is by far the best.

however, are either too small, too slick, or poorly placed and do not allow the knife to be thumbed open reliably. Many of the more substantial studs offer a good thumb purchase, but, like the Flicket, are hard on your pockets. Large studs can also snag during a draw.

Since hand sizes and thumb lengths vary greatly from person to person, if you're shopping for a knife with a thumb stud, try it out at a store before you buy. If a particular knife doesn't open well for you after 20 or 30 tries, keep looking.

Katz brand knives and some folder designs produced by Benchmade knives use a disk fastened to the back of the blade rather than a stud to provide a leverage point for the thumb. Disks have the advantage of being ambidextrous and offering somewhat better leverage than studs but are often too small and difficult to find when you're in a hurry.

The best solution to the problem of offering a good thumb purchase is the patented blade hole found on knives made by Spyderco of Golden, Colorado. The Spyderco design is as simple as it is brilliant. Rather than adding a stud or attachment to the blade, they simply bored a countersunk hole through it. This hole provides an excellent purchase for both the left and right hands and is snag-free. It also offers the advantage of being able to cut all the way through or thrust all the way into something without the blade snagging on a protruding thumb stud. For obvious reasons, this is an important bonus for personal defense knives.

The lockback-style knives offered by Spyderco also feature a forward lock design, which reduces the spring tension on the blade, making quick openings even easier. Additionally, many of their designs are offered with lightweight Zytel plastic handles, which decrease the knife's weight and its magnetic signature (making them easier to carry through metal detectors). These lightweight handles also shift the blade-to-handle weight ratio in favor of the blade, making inertia openings much easier.

While singing the praises of Spyderco, I should also mention that it was the first company to promote serrated blades as practical working blades. Its patented Spyderedge serration pattern is offered on all its models and has been very well received by police and rescue workers, who often use it to cut auto accident victims out of seat belts. It is also popular among sailors, who frequently use their knives to cut rope. Against fibrous materials (especially clothing and flesh), serrated blades cut much more aggressively than straight edges. As you may recall, the longer the cutting edge of a blade, the deeper and more effectively it will cut when drawn across a target. The teeth on a serrated blade greatly increase the linear surface of the cutting edge, so it's no wonder that they cut so well. Wounds produced by serrated blades also tend to be more ragged and thus do not close as well as cuts from straight edges. Against an attacker with a heavy coat, a good serrated edge is second only to the chopping power of a big Bowie knife but remains a hell of a lot easier to carry.

The design innovations made by Spyderco have not been ignored by other cutlery manufacturers. Gerber Legendary Blades, through a licensing agreement with Spyderco, developed its E-Z Out folder. This knife features an elliptical blade hole for easy opening, a Zytel synthetic handle with Kraton rubber inserts for a sure grip, and a stainless-steel pocket clip.

Likewise, Benchmade knives has introduced its excellent AFCK (Advanced Folding Combat Knife), a folder specifically designed for defensive applications by Chris Caracci, director of the edged weapons course at the famed Gunsite Training Center. This knife is available in two sizes with either a standard edge or optional 50/50 edge with Spyderedge serrations on the rear half of the blade. A liner lock design, this knife has handle scales made of a special high-pressure laminate and is shaped to provide a very secure combat grip. One-handed opening is accomplished with the patented Spyderco blade hole. Imitation remains the sincerest form of flattery.

THE BLADE GRIP/HANDLE SWING OPENING

Another method of opening a standard lockblade folder with one hand is accomplished by holding the closed knife upside down between your thumb and fingers with the back of the blade facing your palm. Grip the blade firmly between your thumb and index finger and snap your wrist downward. The weight of the handle will cause it to pivot downward until the knife locks open. Now adjust your grip on the handle of the knife.

Like the thumb opening, this method requires that a good portion of the blade be exposed when the knife is closed. This opening can be used with knives equipped with blade studs, however, do not attempt to grip the blade by the stud only. You retain better control of the knife by gripping the blade directly and are much less likely to drop it when you snap your wrist.

Of all the folding knife designs available, Spyderco knives and licensed copies featuring blade holes are the best suited for this technique. The hole in the blade allows the best possible purchase for the thumb and forefinger since the fingers can actually touch each other through the hole.

THE RING FINGER OPENING

If your personal knife fighting style favors a reverse grip (with the blade extending from the little finger side of the hand), the ring finger opening is a good choice. This opening

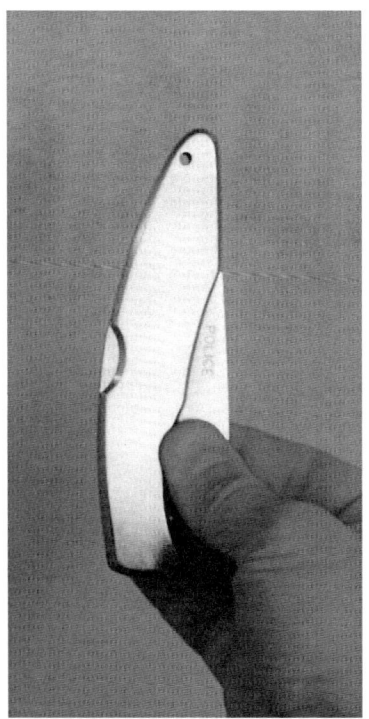
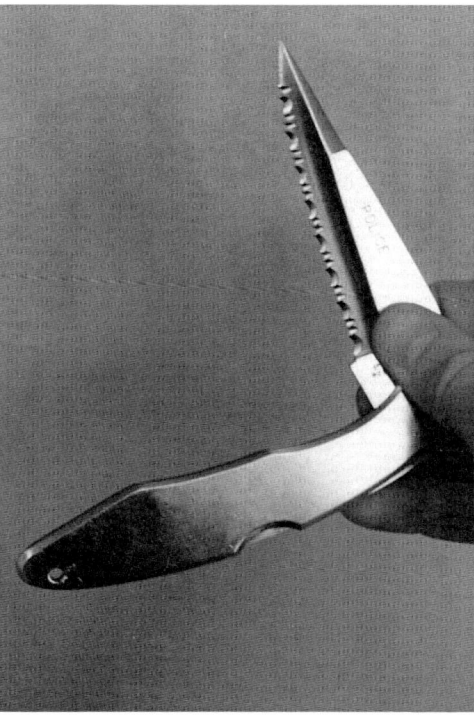
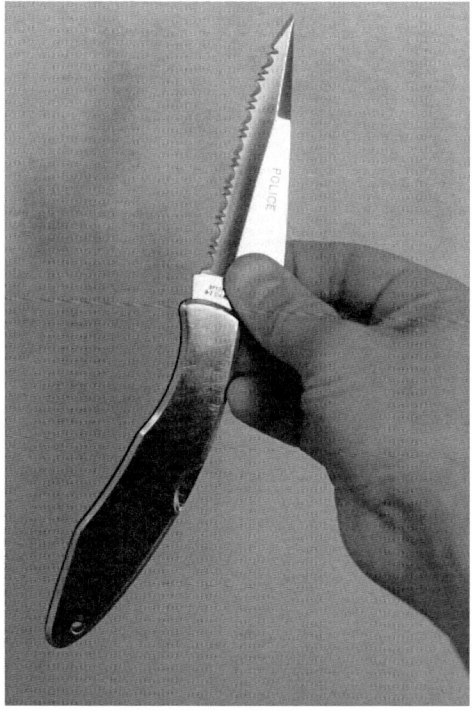

The blade grip/handle swing opening is done by gripping the exposed back of the blade between the thumb and forefinger and pointing the butt end of the closed knife upward. From here a quick downward snap of the wrist swings the handle down and locks the knife in the open position. This method is the best one-handed opening for conventional folders that do not have thumb studs or holes.

Opening Folding Knives One-Handed

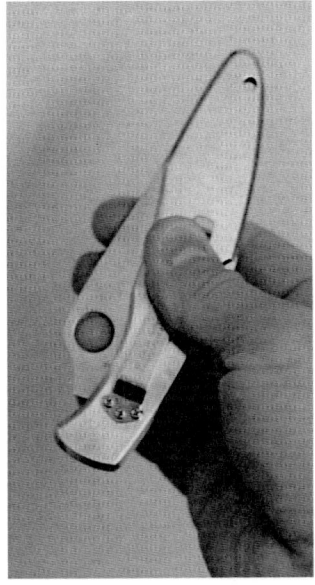 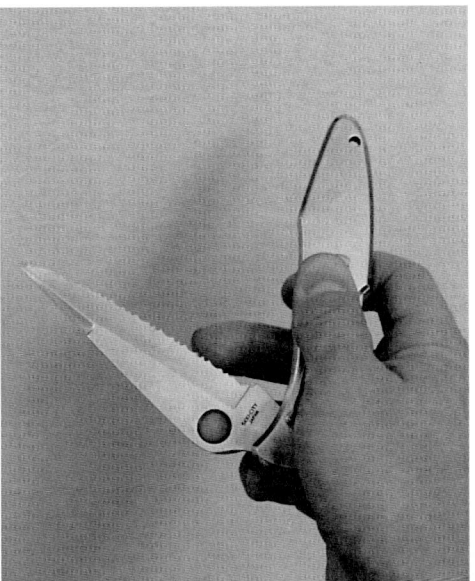 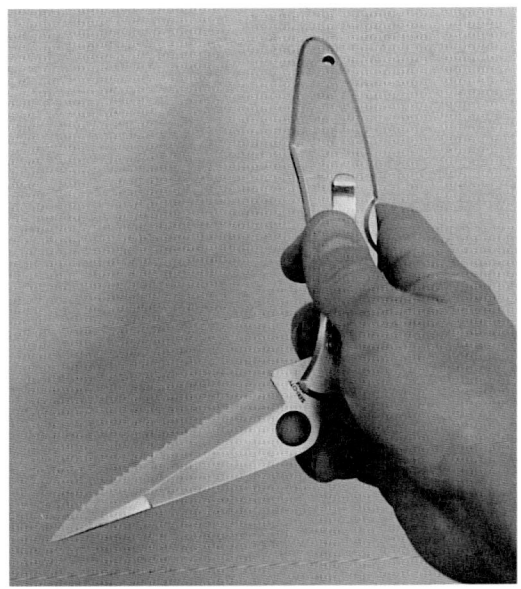

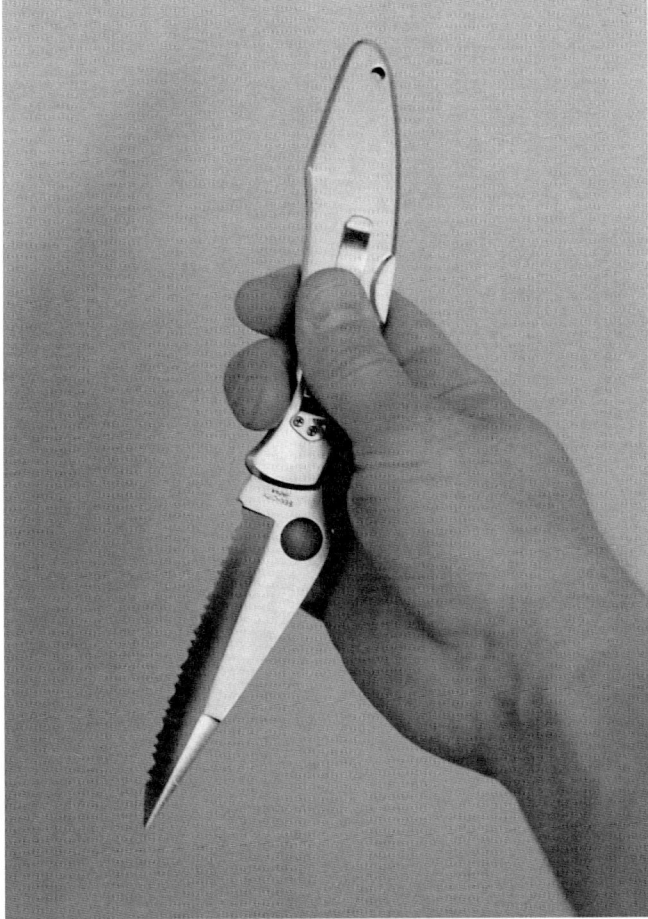

The ring finger opening works very much like the thumb opening with the ring finger doing all the work. The key to doing this opening well is gripping close to the pivot pin end of the handle to ensure that the ring finger can extend the blade all the way to the open position. This is an excellent opening for knife fighters who prefer the reverse grip.

works much like the thumb opening, except the knife is reversed in the hand and the ring finger does all the work. Grip the closed knife between your thumb and fingers with the butt facing up and the blade facing away from your palm. With your ring finger, push against the nail nick, blade stud, or blade hole to begin the opening of the blade. As the blade continues to open, shift the pressure of your finger so it guides the blade around in an arc until fully open. Like the thumb opening, this opening can also be combined with an inertial opening. When your ring finger has opened the blade about 30 degrees, snap your wrist downward to complete the opening.

GRAVITY/INERTIA OPENINGS

According to federal, state, and local laws concerning switchblades, a knife that can be opened with a "flick of the wrist" is considered illegal. In many areas, the concealed carry of such a knife is a felony. In reality, a great number of the commercial folding knives that are sold openly in knife shops across the country and are carried daily by millions of Americans can be opened with a flick of the wrist.

Those who carry knives for personal defense must remember that knife laws are imprecise and easily manipulated. If the legally carried folding knife you used in legitimate self-defense suddenly becomes an illegal weapon in the eyes of the court, the tables can turn on you very quickly. My advice is to learn the techniques that follow, master them, and be prepared to use them in your own defense. Do not, however, display your knife-opening skills to the public, the police, or the court.

The most important thing to understand about inertia openings is that, since the knife's pivot pin is the axis on which the blade opens, it must also be the axis of your hand movement. When most people first try inertia openings, they flail their entire arm. As they get more frustrated, the flailings become more violent, more exaggerated, and less effective. In reality, opening a folder with inertia requires a *rotation* of the wrist rather than a linear snap. This is not only less physically demanding, it can be done in a very confined space.

To do an inertia opening with a standard grip, hold your closed knife between the tips of

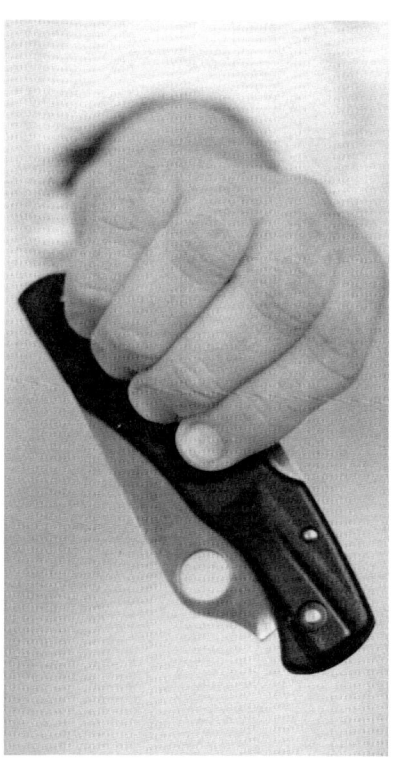  

Many folding knives, especially liner locks and rocker lock knives with short locking bars, can be opened by inertia alone. To do this with a standard grip, hold the knife tightly with your fingertips and turn your palm downward until the elbow of your knife arm begins to rise. Now quickly rotate your hand to a palm-up position, keeping the knife's pivot pin at the center of the rotation. Do not whip your arm or allow your hand to move more than an inch or two from its original position. Done properly, this technique allows you to open a wide variety of perfectly legal folding knives as fast as a good switchblade and with the same intimidating effect.

Opening Folding Knives One-Handed

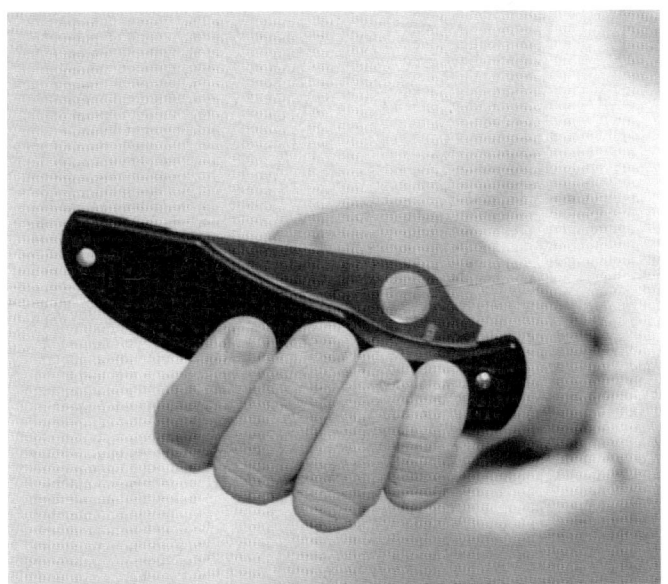

The inertia opening can also be performed with a reverse grip. Begin by gripping the knife tightly with your finger tips with the tip of your little finger very near the pivot pin of the knife. Turn your hand palm up. Now quickly rotate your hand to the palm-down position, keeping the knife's pivot pin at the center of the rotation. Again, your hand should not move from its position; it should only rotate.

your four fingers and thumb with the pivot pin up and the blade facing away from your palm. Your thumb should be about 1 to 1 1/2 inches below the pivot pin. Now turn your hand downward until the palm faces out and your elbow rises slightly (if you are doing this right-handed, your hand will turn counterclockwise). From this position, rapidly turn your hand back to the original position *rotating it around an axis centered on the pivot pin of the knife*. When this is done quickly, your hand will actually go past the starting position into a palm-up position where it should stop abruptly to create a snap. If your knife didn't open completely but you heard the blade click slightly, you're on the right track. Keep trying and continue to focus on a rotational movement rather than a linear snap.

As mentioned earlier, inertia techniques work best (and are easiest to learn) with knives that have lightweight handles. They are also best suited for use with forward lock or liner lock knives, since these designs apply minimal pressure on the blade when the knife is in the closed position. Inertia techniques are very

63

difficult if not impossible to perform with heavy-handled folders with full-length locking bars.

To do a reverse-grip inertia opening, grip your closed knife between the tips of your fingers and thumb with the butt upward and the blade facing away from your palm. The tip of your little finger should be directly over the pivot pin. Turn your hand so that the palm faces upward (clockwise, if you are gripping the knife with the right hand), then quickly rotate your hand back downward *around the axis of the tip of your little finger* and stop with an abrupt snap. This opening is actually a little easier to learn than the standard grip opening, so you might want to try it first.

One final note on opening folding knives one handed: No matter how much you practice, things can still go wrong. If you find yourself in deep shit and your one-handed technique just isn't happening, bring your other hand into play and open the knife. If your other hand is injured or otherwise occupied, thumb your blade open just enough to get the blade point to clear the handle and hook the point on your belt, pants, or anything else that won't bleed and use it to open your knife. When all else fails, you can even use your teeth to pull the blade open.

BALISONGS

In addition to standard folding knife designs, there are a number of atypical designs that are well suited to one-handed openings and personal defense. One of the best is the balisong, or Filipino butterfly knife. Rather than a single handle, this design features two handles that rotate in opposite directions around the blade, completely enclosing it when the knife is closed and exposing it and locking it rigidly into place when the knife is open.

The beauty of the balisong design is that it allows more than 20 different one-handed opening techniques. Complete instruction in these techniques is beyond the scope of this book but is available in my videotape *Mastering the Balisong Knife*, also from Paladin Press. Besides, though there are many ways of opening the balisong, only a few are suitable for use during or immediately prior to a fight. For the sake of simplicity, I will explain only two openings here.

The basic balisong opening technique for the standard grip is the upward swing opening. Grasp the knife in a standard grip and release the locking latch with your little finger. Now turn the knife (if necessary) so the safe handle (the handle into which the unsharpened edge of the blade folds) is against your palm and your palm is turned down. Swing the free handle (the handle into which the sharpened edge of the blade folds) upward toward the back of your hand. As the free handle nears your knuckles, grip the underside of the safe handle with your fingers and point your thumb outward to clear a path for the free handle. When the free handle reaches the end of its upward arc and strikes the safe handle, close your hand and complete your grip. On "Batangas-style" knives, which have the locking latch secured to the free handle, your completed grip will leave the blade edge facing upward. Depending upon your knife-fighting style, you may prefer to turn the knife in the hand to face the edge downward.

The best reverse-grip combat opening is the reverse forward swing opening. Hold the balisong inverted (butt end up) with the safe handle in the crotch of your thumb and your thumb pressing the closed knife against your curled fingers. Release the locking latch with your thumb and let the free handle fall forward. As it continues its arc, curl your fingers around the slotted side of the safe handle and point your thumb out to clear a path for the free handle. Continue the arc of the free handle upward until it meets the safe handle, then close your hand to complete the grip. As you complete your grip, rotate the knife so the edge of the blade faces away from you.

If you decide to carry a balisong for personal defense, plan your carry carefully so that you can automatically identify and grasp the safe handle. With some openings, grabbing

Opening Folding Knives One-Handed

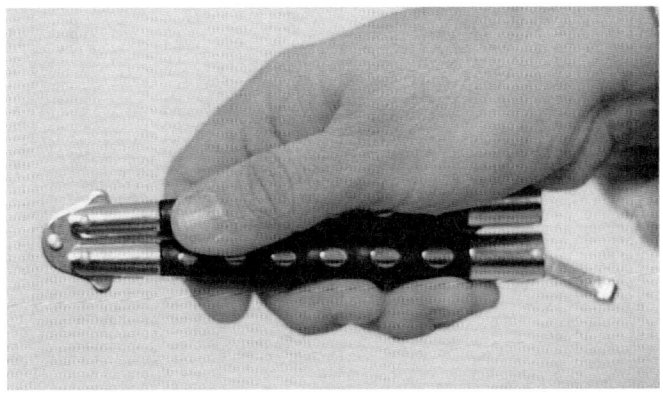

the wrong handle could cause a serious cut and even make you drop your knife—not a good way to go into a fight.

Also, if you elect to use a balisong as your carry knife, bear in mind that it is considered by many law enforcement agencies to be a type of switchblade and is illegal in some areas. Again, a trip to your local library will help you learn what types of knives are generally considered legal in your area.

BARRY WOOD KNIVES

Another atypical folding knife design that could be used for self-defense was designed by

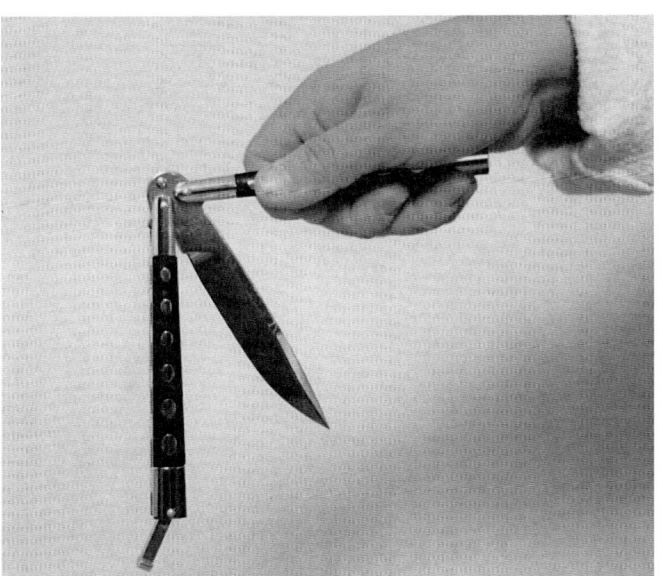

There are many methods of opening a balisong one-handed. The most reliable standard grip opening is the upward swing. After releasing the locking latch with your little finger, hold the safe handle (the handle into which the unsharpened back of the blade folds) against your palm with your palm down. Release the free handle and blade and swing them upward toward you. As the free handle nears the back of your hand, curl your fingers under the slotted side of the safe handle and point your thumb out. Allow the free handle to complete its arc and grip both handles together.

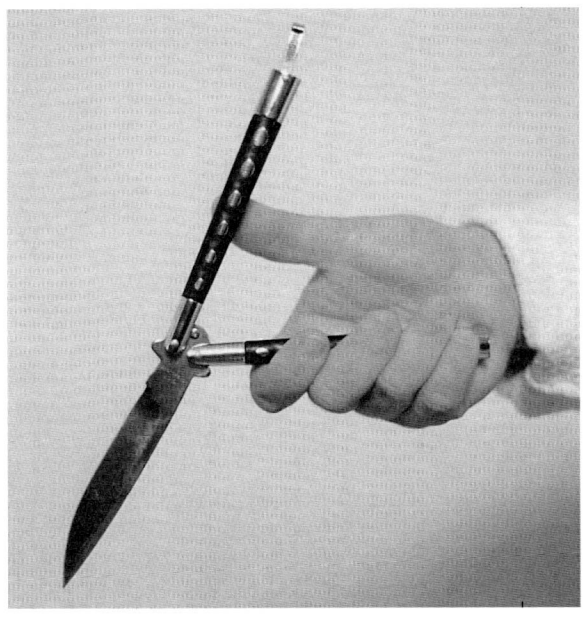
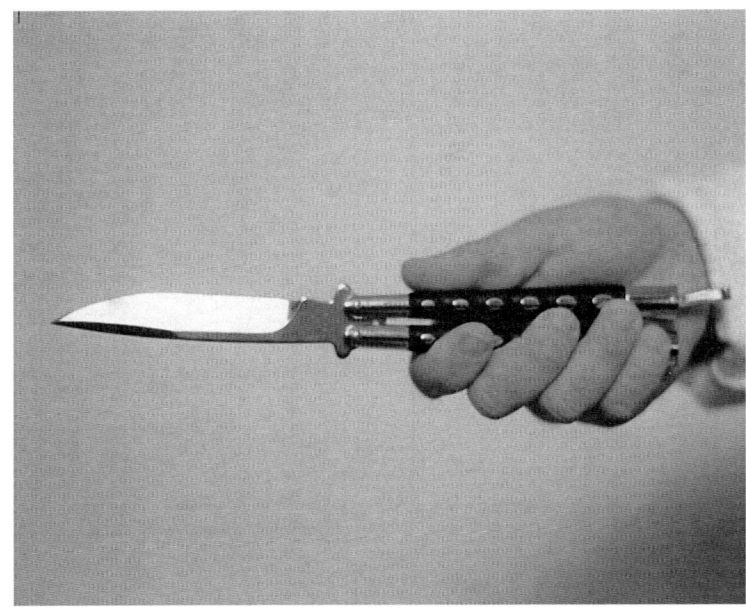

The reverse forward swing opening is a quick and reliable reverse-grip opening. Release the locking latch with your thumb so the closed knife is held in a reverse grip with the safe handle against your palm. Release the free handle and blade and swing them forward and downward. As the free handle hits the bottom of its arc, curl your fingers around the slotted side of the safe handle and point your thumb out. Swing the free handle upward until it strikes the safe handle, then complete your grip.

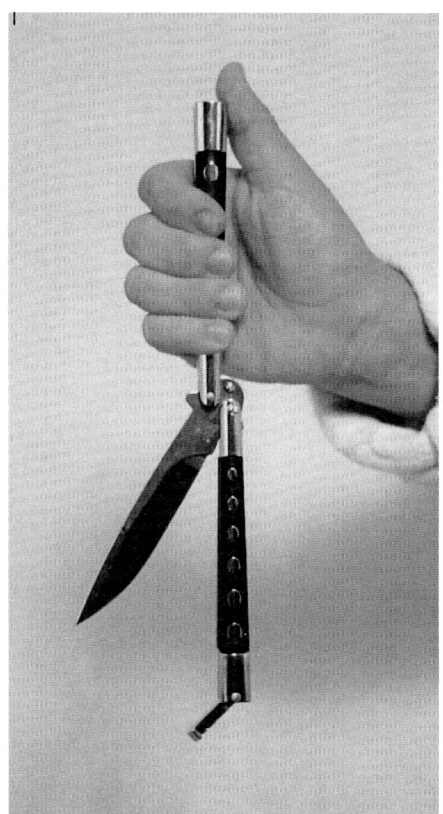

knifemaker Barry Wood. This is also a twin handle design, but the handles pivot on a single pivot pin. When one handle scale is rotated 180 degrees, it engages the blade and rotates it outward. Rotating that handle scale another 180 degrees completely exposes the blade and locks it in place.

This style of knife can be opened with one hand, but it can only be done *safely* with the right hand. Left-handed openings place the hand precariously close to the knife edge and are therefore not recommended.

To open a Barry Wood-style knife one-handed, grip the closed knife in the palm of your hand with the pivot pin over the base of your index finger and the blade back facing your thumb. Press the tips of your four fingers against the bottom handle scale while pushing the blade back with your thumb. This will separate the bottom scale

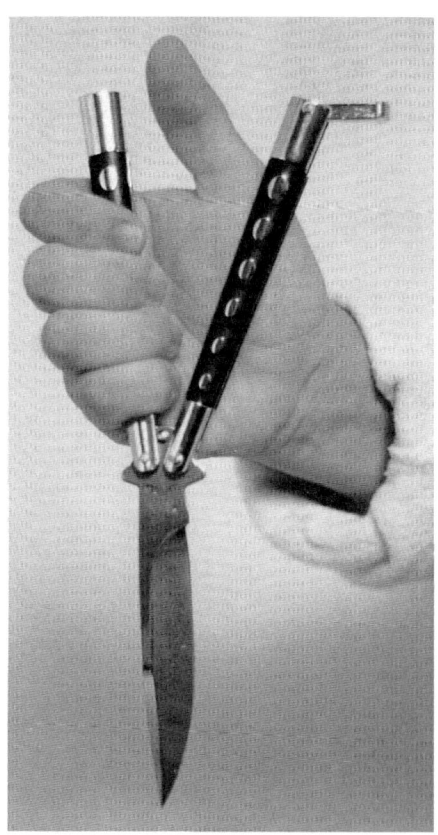
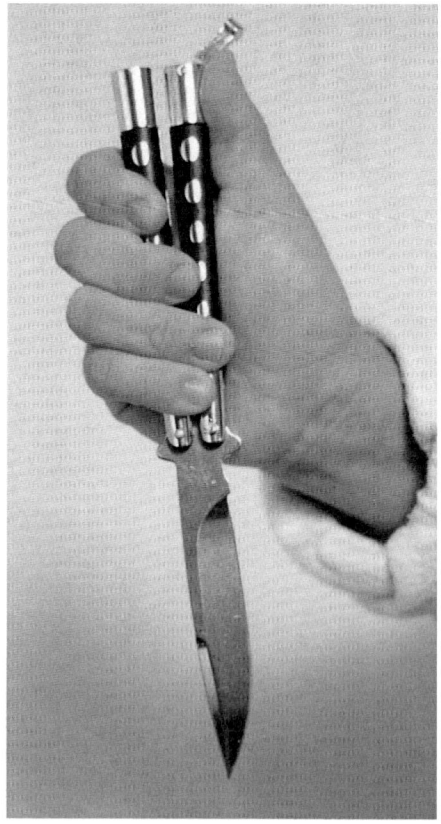

If you carry a folder for self-defense, you should practice your one-handed openings until they become second nature, because you may not have time to think when you really need your knife. Here an attacker armed with a hammer makes the mistake of extending his lead hand. The defender quickly grabs the attacker's fingers and wrenches them downward. From this position, the defender executes a well-practiced draw and one-handed opening while monitoring the attacker and angling away from his weapon. Once the knife is out, it is used to bring a quick, albeit bloody end to the confrontation. This scenario also reinforces the need to develop your unarmed defensive skills for use in conjunction with your knife.

and begin rotating the blade and top scale clockwise. Continue pushing the blade back with your thumb and rotate it and the top handle scale 180 degrees. At this point, the blade will stop. Now curl your fingers around the bottom scale and use your thumb to push the top handle scale an additional 90 degrees while you turn the knife edge down and begin assuming a standard grip. Finally, reach up with your index finger and pull the top handle scale the rest of the way down to meet the bottom scale and complete your grip.

To close the knife one-handed, grip it in a standard grip with the blade edge facing to the left. With your thumb, pull to the right on the top scale as you push to the left with your fingers on the bottom scale. This will separate the handles. Gripping the top scale with your ring and little fingers, use a pincer action of your thumb and index finger to close the blade and bottom scale together and cover the sharp edge of the knife. When this is done, the blade and bottom scale should be at a 180-degree position from the top scale. Now push the bottom scale and blade 90 degrees to the right (clockwise) with your thumb, then reach up with your index finger and continue the clockwise rotation to the closed position.

Custom-made Barry Wood knives are available with a variety of options from Barry Wood and Michael Irie of Colorado Springs,

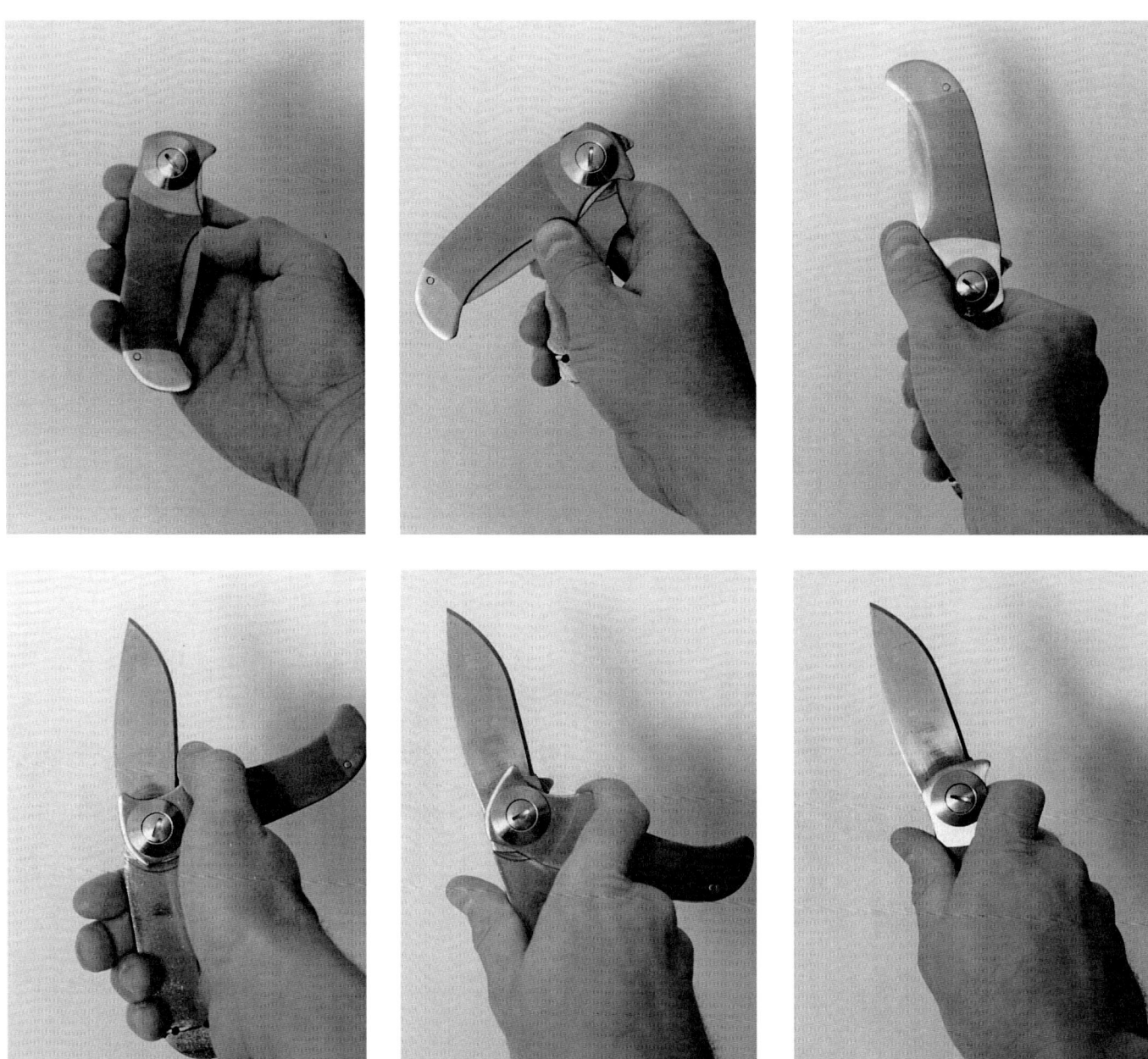

Opening a Barry Wood-style folder one-handed takes a bit of dexterity and practice. Begin by gripping the knife with your thumb on the back of the blade. Push the blade and top handle with your thumb to separate them from the bottom handle. Then rotate the top handle and blade clockwise with your thumb. At 180 degrees, the blade will stop. Continue to rotate the top handle to 270 degrees, then use your index finger to pull the top handle the rest of the way to the open position.

OPENING FOLDING KNIVES ONE-HANDED

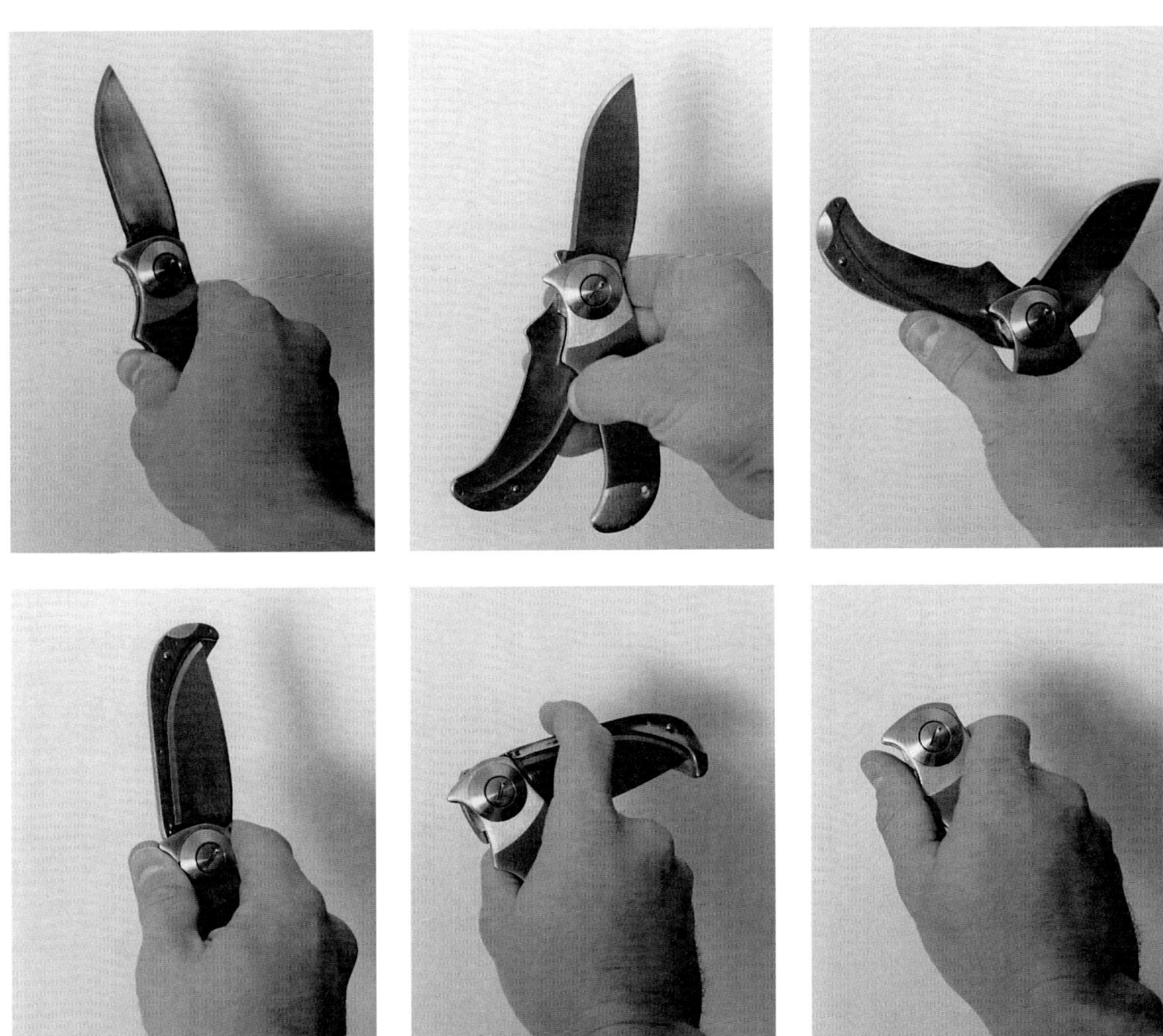

Closing a Barry Wood folder one-handed begins by holding the open knife with the edge facing to the left. With a push-pull action of the thumb and fingers, separate the handles and push the bottom handle clockwise. Gripping the top handle with the middle, ring, and little fingers, use the thumb and index finger to close the blade and bottom handle with a pincer movement. Finally, use the index finger to rotate the blade and bottom handle clockwise to the closed position.

Colorado. A number of other custom makers, including Scot Horton of Buhl, Idaho, also offer this design. During the mid to late 1980s, Benchmade Knives of Clackamas, Oregon, produced a commercial version of this design that can still be found for sale if you look hard enough. The Wyoming Knife Company of Ft. Collins, Colorado, also offers this design in the form of its Powder River folding knives.

Although one of the slower one-handed openers, the Barry Wood design is very strong and remains a good choice as a defensive knife.

MANUAL OUT-THE-FRONT KNIVES

One unique style of one-handed folding knife does not actually fold at all. Instead, the blade slides out the front of the handle in a linear fashion, propelled by pressure from the thumb.

The first design of this type was produced and marketed by the Benchmark Knife Company. They offered two basic models, the Sidewinder and the Diamondback, featuring the unique Rolox system designed by Blackie Collins. With this system, the serrated rear portion of the blade is pushed downward with the thumb to raise the blade tip and free the blade to slide forward. The thumb then pushes the blade all the way forward to the open position, where it is locked firmly in place by a locking bar located on the underside of the handle. An ingenious design, this knife was produced with a number of handle scale options and provided with a high-quality form-fitting belt pouch.

Benchmark was ultimately purchased by Gerber, and the Rolox design was modified to make it cheaper and easier to produce. Versions of this design are offered with molded Lexan handles, which, though not as attractive as the Micarta and stag featured on the original Benchmark products, are nevertheless very durable.

Another out-the-front design is the Bokermatic, a product of Boker Knives, Solingen, Germany, imported by Boker USA.

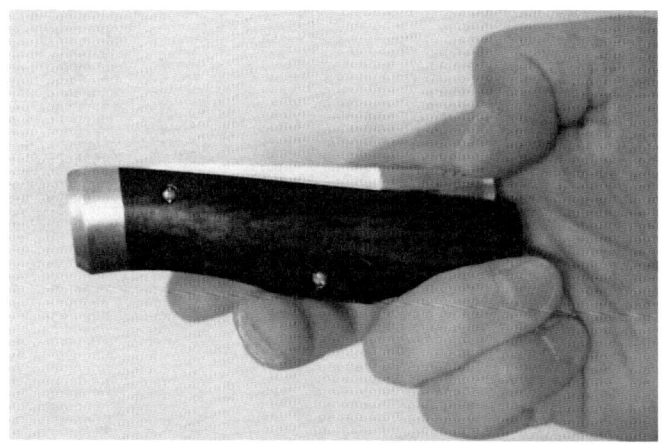

The blade of the Benchmark Diamondback does not fold but slides out the front of the handle. To open this knife, depress the serrated base of the blade with your thumb until the point of the blade rises. Then use your thumb to push the blade all the way forward to the locked position.

OPENING FOLDING KNIVES ONE-HANDED

 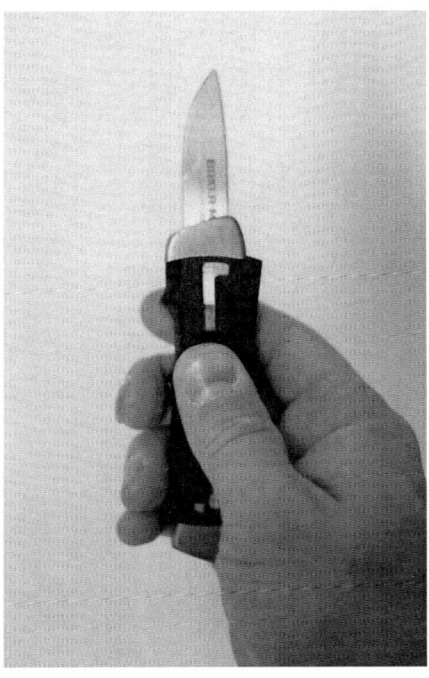 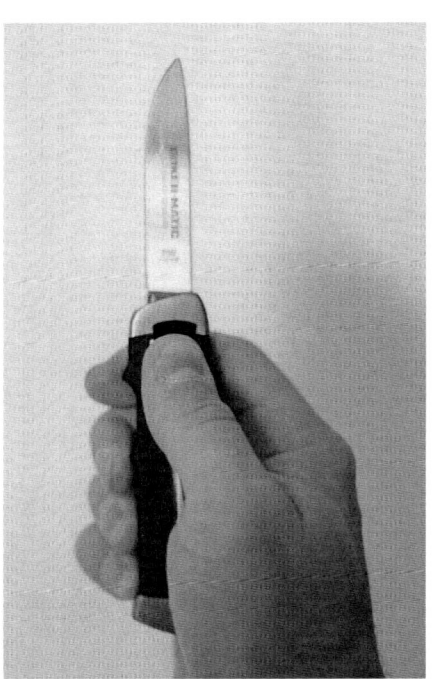

To open the Bokermatic knife, twist the slotted handle scale counterclockwise to line up the thumb button with the longitudinal slot in the scale. Then use your thumb to push the thumb button all the way forward, exposing the blade. Tightening your grip on the handle will snap the slotted handle scale back into place, locking the blade open. Although this is a unique design that can be opened quickly, it is fairly fragile and not a good choice for a full-duty defensive blade.

This knife features a slim stainless-steel blade that slides within a stainless and nickel silver handle. Attached to the base of the blade is a thumb button that extends through a slotted handle scale made of durable synthetic. The slot in this handle is in the shape of an elongated backward letter "Z" and serves as the knife's locking mechanism. When the handle scale is rotated slightly, the thumb button is aligned with the long section of the handle slot. The thumb then pushes the button forward, extending the blade out the front of the knife. When the blade is fully extended, the handle scale is rotated back into place, locking the blade open. The extension of the blade is accomplished against the tension of a spring, so that when the handle scale is again rotated to align the long section of the slot with the thumb button, the blade quickly snaps back into the handle. Care should be taken to keep the fingers well clear of the edge when doing this to prevent being cut as the blade retracts into the handle.

Although an interesting and innovative design, the Bokermatic does not have a durable enough locking mechanism to qualify as a full-service defensive knife. As a "slash and dash" weapon it will suffice, but I would not count on it in a serious encounter.

OTHER ONE-HANDED KNIVES

A number of years ago, a custom knifemaker named Paul Poehlmann designed a unique folding knife with a push-button locking system. The lock mechanism was built into the pivot pin of the knife and locked the blade very securely into place in both the closed and open positions.

Gerber Legendary Blades licensed the design from Poehlmann and produced a commercial version called simply the Paul

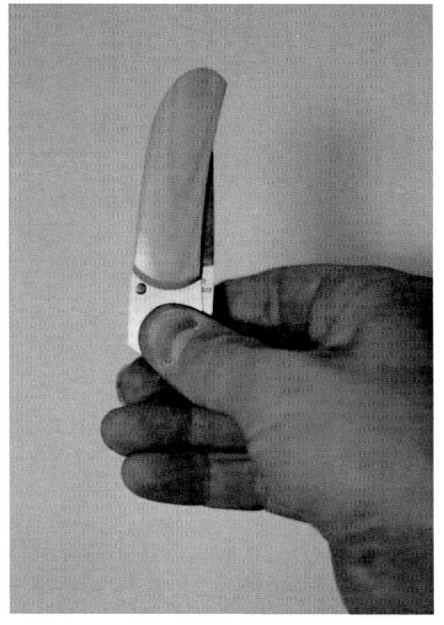  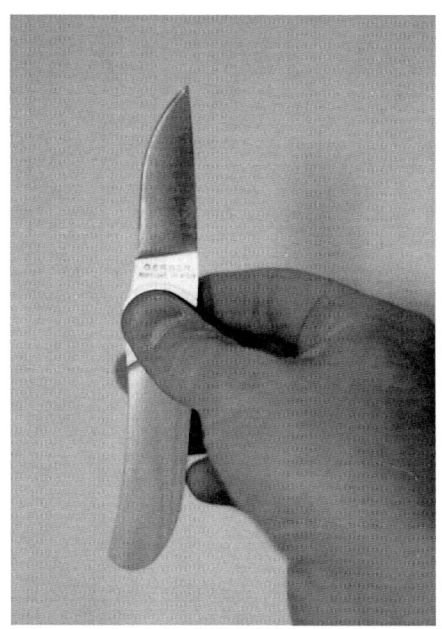

Opening a Paul knife one-handed is done by pinching the locking button between your thumb and forefinger with the back of the blade facing the crotch of your thumb and the butt end of the handle facing upward. Squeezing the locking button will release the handle and allow you to swing it downward. Releasing the button will lock the blade open.

knife. Although a bit small for a defensive blade, this knife nevertheless offered a practical, easily carried blade that could be opened very quickly with one hand. Gerber stopped production of these a few years ago, so Paul knives have become collector's items of sorts. Gerber reintroduced the design in late 1995.

Custom versions of the Paul knife were also available during the late 1970s and early 1980s. Although expensive, the custom versions could be had in larger sizes that were more suitable for defensive use. Paul Poehlmann is not listed in any of the annual custom knifemaking summaries after 1986, so I assume that his knives are no longer available.

If you are lucky enough to own or purchase a Paul knife, here's how to open it one-handed: Hold the knife by pinching the lock button between your thumb and forefinger with the knife inverted (butt end up) and the blade back facing you. Now depress the lock button with your thumb and swing the handle forward and down. When the knife is fully opened, release the lock button and close your hand to complete your grip.

For a number of years, Tekna also produced a knife with a push-button lock. Called the Hidden Edge, this folder was a very light knife with a cut-out blade and an all-synthetic handle. By depressing the push-button lock, you could snap open the knife very quickly with a flick of the wrist. Releasing the button locked the blade in the open position. Although a unique design that could be opened very quickly, this knife is too small and fragile to trust in a fight. This knife is no longer in production but can still occasionally be found for sale in knife shops.

One folder design that works very well as a gravity knife is Gerber's Bolt Action. Bolt Action folders lock their blades both open and closed via a spring-loaded stainless-steel bolt that slides lengthwise in a cavity in the knife's synthetic handle. A button attached to the bolt allows it to be retracted with the thumb to unlock the blade. When the bolt is released, a spring drives the bolt forward to lock the blade.

By retracting the bolt on these knives and

snapping your wrist sharply, you will find that you have a very functional gravity knife. Bolt-Action knives are available at very reasonable prices in a variety of configurations and blade profiles. There are even models that feature interchangeable blades, offering a variety of blade styles with a single knife handle.

Cold Steel offers a variety of knife designs well suited for a personal-defense role. Many of its folding designs incorporate blade opening studs, but its most unusual one-handed folders are found in its Ultralock series.

Available in a clip-point, serrated clip-point, and tanto-point blade styles, Ultralock folders at first appear to be rather conventional liner lock folding knives. If you look a bit closer, however, you'll see that the rear portion of the blade back and the exposed edge of the blade tang have a series of serrations. When you grip the closed knife in a standard grip with the blade away from the palm, the thumb falls naturally on top of the blade tang. Rubbing downward against the serrations with the same motion used to light a butane lighter quickly rotates the blade to the open, locked position. This can be done equally well with either hand. Called the Thumbglide™ system, this design is free of any studs or disks that can interfere with cutting or thrusting penetration. It cannot be operated reliably with the ring finger to produce a reverse-grip opening, however. Reverse-grip openings with this knife are restricted to inertia openings.

There is also the Lev-R-Lock knife, produced by Soque River Knives of Clarksville, Georgia. This is an innovative design that incorporates a lever-operated quick opening device into an otherwise conventional lockback folder. By depressing an external lever on the handle of the knife with your thumb, the blade is lifted and rotated to the open position. Though an ingenious and sturdy design, as a defensive blade, this knife suffers from its small size and the fact that the lever can only be operated with the right hand. The lever could also interfere with some combat-grip styles.

AUTOMATIC KNIVES AND GRAVITY KNIVES

Automatic knives, or "autos," are knives that open by spring pressure against the blade. More commonly known as switchblades, these knives are now called "automatics" by cutlery buffs in an attempt to reestablish them as legitimate and respectable pieces of bladeware. Prior to the late 1950s, automatic knives were as common and accepted as any other type of knife. When youth gangs began to become more popular and the image of the switchblade-wielding juvenile delinquent was immortalized on the silver screen, lawmakers, in the time-honored tradition of banning inanimate objects rather than punishing criminals for their acts, passed laws against automatic knives.

Not surprisingly, the laws prohibiting switchblade knives have done little to curb juvenile crime. As such, the attitude toward the enforcement of these ill-conceived laws has generally become lax, and these once-scarce knives have gradually become easier to find. A few years ago, the Edge Knife Company began offering switchblade "kits" through the mail, thinly veiling its efforts to circumvent laws prohibiting the sale of auto knives. Oregon's switchblade law was openly challenged in court, found unconstitutional, and repealed. This paved the way for the first domestic commercial production of switchblade knives since the 1950s and the introduction of a whole new generation of high-tech auto openers.

Unlike many of the switchblades available prior to the ban, which could not be counted on to withstand the abuse of a serious cut or thrust, today's auto-openers are made to exacting tolerances from high-grade steels, alloys, and synthetics. The quality and strength of these knives easily matches that of conventional folding designs, and the fact that they can be opened instantly by persons with

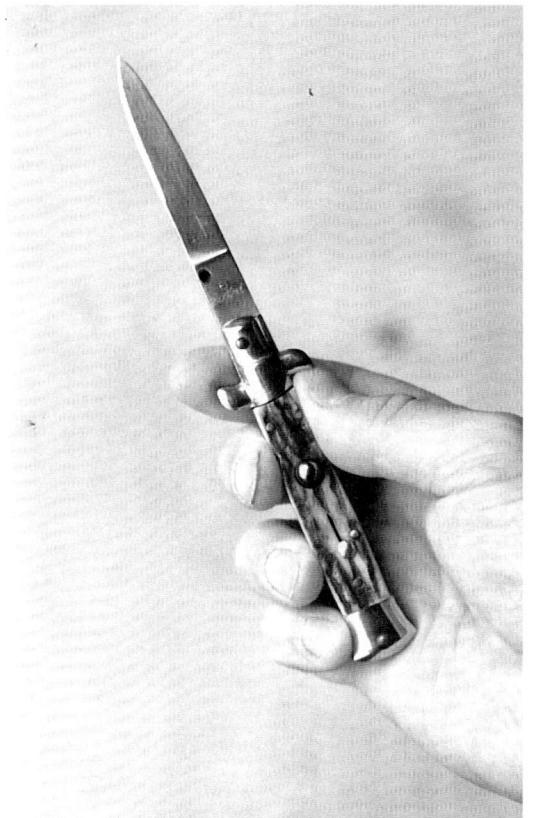

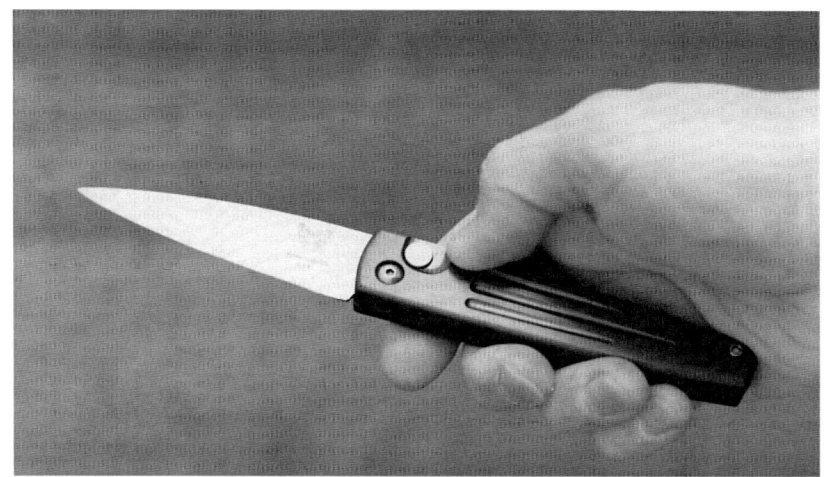

Traditional switchblade designs (left) often suffer from sloppy tolerances and poor construction. As such, they are not reliable weapons in a fight. The new generation of high-tech "automatic" knives (below), however, includes a significant number of combat-worthy designs.

little or no training makes them well-suited for defensive use.

Despite the tactical advantages offered by modern automatic knives, the fact remains that the concealed carry of a switchblade knife is still illegal in most states. If a police officer finds an auto knife on your person during a casual search or traffic stop, he'll most likely confiscate it and give you a warning. However, if you use a switchblade to defend yourself, *even in cases where self-defense was clearly justified*, you could find yourself facing some serious weapons charges.

Of course, you may well find yourself facing charges if you use a fixed blade boot knife or any other knife in self-defense, but the fact that switchblades are easily categorized and specific laws exist concerning them practically guarantees a legal hassle. Again, *you* must decide how much hassle you're willing to endure.

CHAPTER 5

Carry Options for Folding Knives

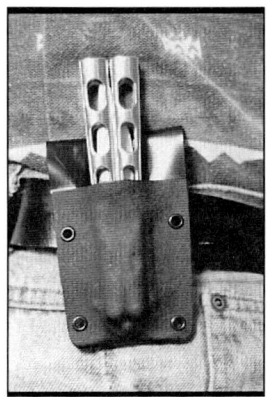

POCKET CARRIES

Folding knives, at least smaller ones, are often referred to as pocket knives. Thus, it's only fitting that the first folding knife carry we discuss is the pocket carry.

Carrying a folding knife in a pocket is a convenient, practical, and low-profile way of packing a personal defense blade. When done properly, with a little bit of forethought, this carry can allow for surprisingly quick draws. When done incorrectly, however, such a carry can promote a false sense of security and make a quick draw nearly impossible.

The first rule when carrying a folder in your pocket is: *Do not carry anything else in that pocket.* Drawing a folding knife in a hurry is a difficult enough task without having to sort through a bunch of other junk to get at it. Keeping your knife alone in a pocket allows you to shove your hand in quickly and get an immediate purchase on it. Anything less simply won't do.

Next you must decide in which pocket you'll carry your knife. Though it's possible to carry a defensive folder in a shirt or coat pocket, unless *all* your shirts are of very similar design with pockets in exactly the same place or you wear the same style of coat all the time, you're better off carrying your knife in a pants pocket. In addition to the fact that pants styles are more uniform than shirt and coat styles, draws from pants pockets tend to be faster because the hand doesn't have to travel as far to access the weapon.

Most styles of pants have two interior front pockets and one or two exterior or "patch" pockets on the rear. Interior pockets have the disadvantage of snagging and turning inside out when you try to remove something from them quickly. Knives also tend to shift in interior pockets, making it difficult to get a predictable grip when you reach for your knife. These pockets are therefore a poor place to carry a knife. Since patch pockets are sewn directly to the base material, they cannot turn inside out and will normally give up a knife without snagging. The fact that most men carry their wallets in their back pockets also makes it possible to draw your knife by feigning a natural move for your wallet, as described in Chapter 3 in the "Object Carries" section.

The problem with carrying a knife in your back pocket is that the pressure on the knife when you sit down tends to wear out the pocket. This is undesirable for two reasons: the outline of your knife prints through the pocket, letting everyone know you're armed, and pants aren't cheap.

You can minimize the wear and tear on your pocket by choosing a knife with a very flat, smooth profile. Although you generally want to get as much of your hand in your pocket as possible to get a firm grasp on your knife before you draw, you can also reduce pocket wear by stitching part of your pocket shut to hold your knife more vertically. This is best done with pants that already have designer pocket stitching, since it gives you a pattern to follow and conceals the alteration. Pants that fit somewhat loosely also tend to minimize pocket wear, as well as making it easier to get your hand into the pocket to initiate a draw.

Once you've chosen a pocket in which to carry your knife, you need to place your knife properly within that pocket. A quick draw can be followed by a quick opening only if you know exactly how the knife is positioned in

This photo shows the proper placement of a folding knife in the back pocket for a thumb opening. In this position, the fingers will curl under the handle as the hand reaches into the pocket, leaving the knife perfectly oriented for a thumb opening or standard grip inertia opening when drawn.

the pocket before you reach for it. In general, you'll want to place your knife in the pocket so you can immediately grasp it in the preopening position. For example, if you prefer a thumb opening with your right hand, your knife should be positioned in your right rear pocket blade down with the handle butt to the left. When you reach into your pocket, your palm will face your body so your fingers and thumb can encircle the knife in a secure standard grip before removing the knife. When your hand clears the pocket, it is already in position on the knife to execute a thumb opening. This positioning also works for a standard grip inertia opening.

If you prefer a blade grip/handle swing

For the blade grip/handle swing opening, the knife must be placed so the back of the blade faces upward and the butt of the knife faces toward the outside of the body. During a draw, the fingers and thumb will grasp the blade back and can begin the opening as soon as the knife clears the pocket.

For reverse-grip openings from a pocket carry, the knife must be positioned with the back of the closed blade facing down and the butt of the handle facing the outside of the body. Drawing is accomplished by grasping the handle in a reverse grip. Once drawn, the knife can be opened with a ring finger opening or a reverse-grip inertia opening.

opening, your knife should be positioned blade up in the pocket with the butt of the handle facing to the right. To draw the knife, reach into your pocket with your palm facing your body and curl your fingers around the knife. As you do this, place your thumb and index finger on opposite sides of the blade back so that as soon as the knife clears the pocket, you can pinch the blade back and flow directly into your opening technique.

For reverse-grip openings, including the ring finger opening and the reverse-grip inertia opening, place the knife blade down in the pocket with the butt facing to the right. Reach into the pocket with your palm facing your body and you will find yourself gripping the knife in a perfect position to execute either of these reverse-grip openings.

Another method of pocket carry is to have a special knife pocket sewn onto your pants. This allows you to take full advantage of your other pockets and gives you the ability to choose the exact location of the pocket to support a specific drawing and opening method. When I was working in Vietnam a few years ago, I had several pairs of work pants made for the occasion. Since Vietnamese laundry facilities—like practically everything else in that country—left something to be desired, I chose a durable

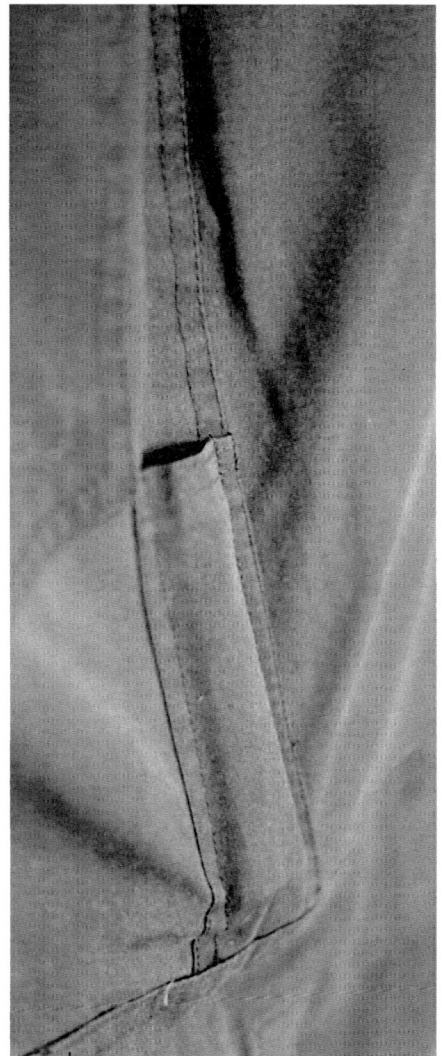 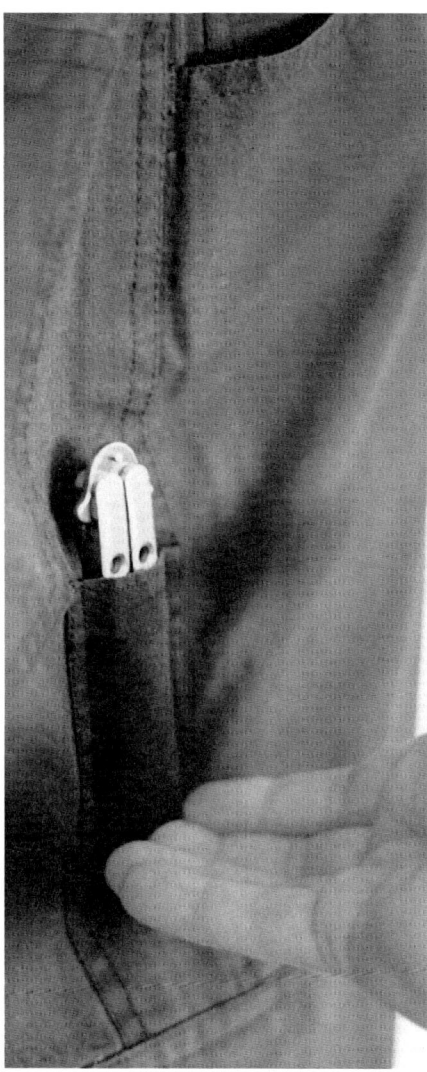 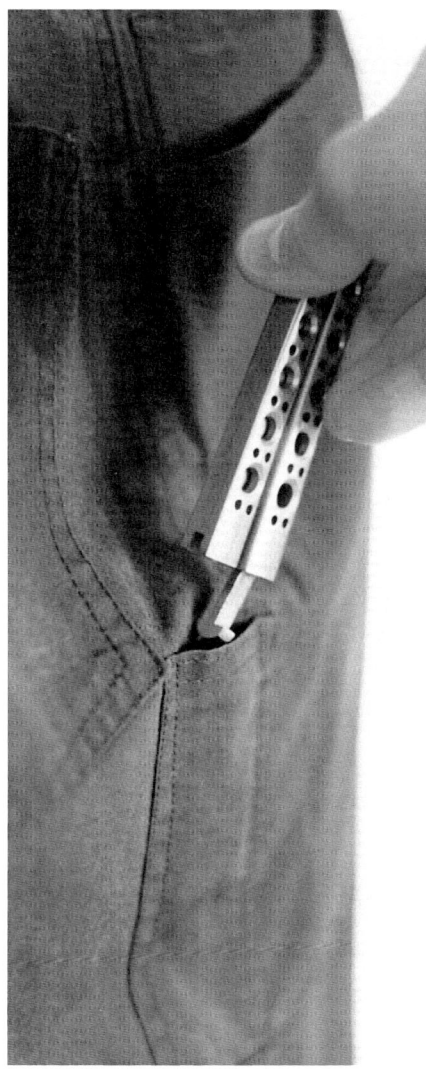

A more expensive carry option is to have special tailored knife pockets added to all your pants. This pocket was specifically designed for the author's Benchmade balisong. Pulling upward from the bottom of the pocket slides the knife up until it is sufficiently exposed to be gripped with the fingers. Note the mouth of the pocket automatically pops the locking latch of the knife upon withdrawal.

permanent press cloth in various shades that hid dirt well. To foil the everpresent Vietnamese pickpockets, I had all the open pockets cut very high to make it difficult to get anything into or out of them, and I had cargo pockets with substantial Velcro closures added to each pants leg.

I also had a knife pocket added to the outer side of the right pant leg so that the bottom of the pocket was even with the tips of my fingers when my hand hung naturally at my side. The dimensions of this narrow vertical pocket were based on the dimensions of my carry knife at the time, a Benchmade balisong with a 3-inch blade. When placed in the pocket butt first, the knife was completely concealed. It also could not fall out, even during rigorous movements such as jumping out of hovering helicopters, falling down mountainsides, and kicking obnoxious cyclo drivers (believe me, I've done them all and still have my knife). However, when I curled my fingers under the pocket and lifted, the knife would slide upward out of the pocket and directly into the grip of my index finger and thumb. As I gained a partial grip on the knife and continued to lift it out of my pocket, the locking latch (which secures the two handles together when the knife is fully open or closed) hooked purposefully on the narrow lip of the pocket and was released just as the knife cleared. This left the knife in perfect position in my hand for a rapid standard-grip opening.

This is just one example of how a special knife pocket can be used to tailor a carry to your specific needs. The disadvantage of this is that you must tailor *all* your pants and shorts to meet this need. Unless you or a close friend are handy with a needle and thread, custom tailoring of this sort can be an expensive proposition.

If you carry a nonstandard folding design as your personal defense knife, there is a simple way to determine how to position it in your pocket. Hold the closed knife in the beginning grip for your preferred one-handed opening technique and simply stick your hand all the way in your pocket. Release the knife, being careful not to let it roll or turn as you remove your hand. Then reinsert your hand and see if you can automatically establish the same grip. If so, note the knife's position and ensure that you place it in your pocket the same way every time.

For example, when I carried a balisong in my back pocket, I preferred a reverse forward swing opening technique. As described earlier, this requires that the knife be gripped butt end up with the safe handle against your palm. For "Batangas-style" knives, which have the locking latch attached to the free handle, the latch is popped with the thumb before the opening begins. Gripping the knife in the preparatory position for this opening and placing it in my right rear pocket, the knife comes to rest with the butt end facing to the right and the safe handle uppermost. By reaching into the pocket with my right hand, palm facing my body, I can instantly establish this grip and open the knife the instant it clears the pocket. As mentioned earlier, being able to index your grip on a balisong the second you grip it is extremely important to avoid cutting yourself when opening the knife one-handed.

One final note on pocket carries: If you carry your defensive blade in a pocket, check and clean it often. Pockets tend to collect all kinds of lint and trash that can prevent your knife from opening and locking properly. By flattening the end of a cotton swab with a pair of pliers and dipping it in alcohol, you can swab the inside of a folder clean in a few minutes. Toothpicks also work well to clean dirt and lint from the locking notches of lockback knives. Once everything is clean, a drop or two of oil or other lubricant will keep the action of your knife slick. Too much oil will actually attract lint and dust, so don't get carried away.

BELT SHEATH CARRIES

Some folding knives are inconvenient and uncomfortable to carry in the pocket. Heavy knives with brass bolsters and large folding knives are usually best carried in a sheath or pouch attached to the belt. However, this carry style, like all others, has distinct advantages and disadvantages that must be considered before you make your choice.

We've already established that folding knives are slower than sheath knives because they require two separate actions to get them into action. Retrieving a folder from your pocket can be done very quickly with practice, since pocket openings are typically large and allow the whole hand access to grip the knife. Belt pouches, though a pocket of sorts, are typically small, offer a limited gripping area on the knife during a draw, and are often secured by snap- or Velcro-fastened flaps that must be released before you can begin your

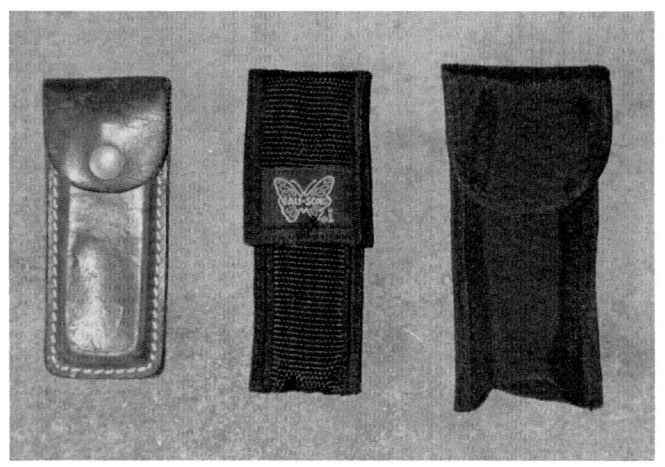

Typical styles of belt pouches for folding knives include snap-fastened leather pouches (left) and Velcro-fastened ballistic nylon pouches (center). The pouch on the right is constructed of thin nylon pack cloth and is a poor second to either of the other styles.

draw. Belt pouches, as the name implies, also require that you *always* wear a belt. There are a number of tricks to speed up the process of liberating your knife from a belt pouch (we'll examine these in a bit), but the fact remains that a draw from a pouch is typically a bit slower than a draw from a pocket.

Carrying a knife in a belt pouch also advertises the fact that you are armed with a knife. This can be both good and bad, depending upon your circumstances. In some jurisdictions, this may be the only way to legally carry a substantial folding knife. In an office environment where a suit and tie are standard or on a college campus, an open carry of this type may be inappropriate.

On the upside, belt pouches eliminate the uncomfortable sensation of a folding knife jabbing you in the ass every time you sit down. They also may be mounted in a variety of carry positions that can make your knife much more accessible than a pocket carry, especially if you spend a lot of time seated or in a vehicle.

Belt pouches come in two basic varieties: leather pouches with snap-fastened flaps and nylon pouches with Velcro-fastened flaps. Both styles, when well designed and made, offer a good compromise between secure carry and quick access. The snap fasteners on leather pouches are quieter than Velcro, allowing you to sneak your knife into your hand more discreetly than with a Velcro-fastened pouch. Snaps also last longer than Velcro, which loses its grip after a couple of years of constant use. Nylon pouches are good because they come in a greater variety of styles than leather pouches and dry out quickly if they become wet.

By the way, when choosing a nylon pouch, especially if ordering by mail, make sure you get one made of "ballistic nylon." This is a heavy nylon weave that is stiff enough to hold its shape and is as durable as leather. Many cheap nylon pouches are made of nylon pack cloth, a much lighter grade of cloth used to make backpacks and the like.

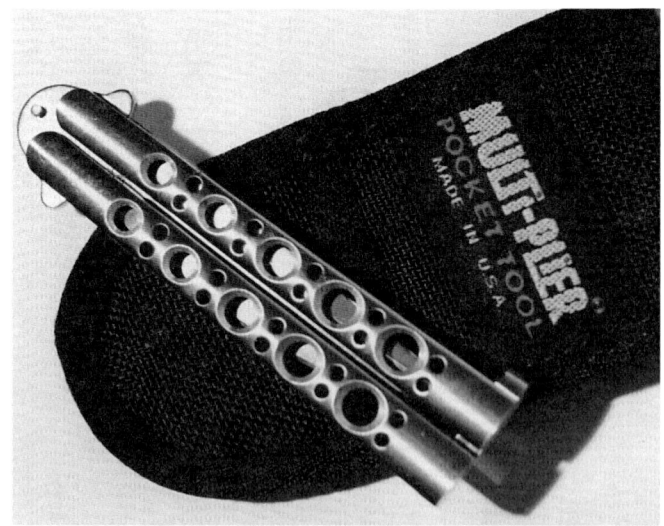

A great way to lower your profile when carrying a defensive folding knife in a belt pouch is to carry it in a pouch made for one of the increasingly popular varieties of folding tools, such as the Gerber Multi-Plier. These tools are becoming so commonplace that the sight of one on a person's belt won't raise any eyebrows. The sight of an exotic folder, such as this Benchmade balisong, would certainly generate much more interest.

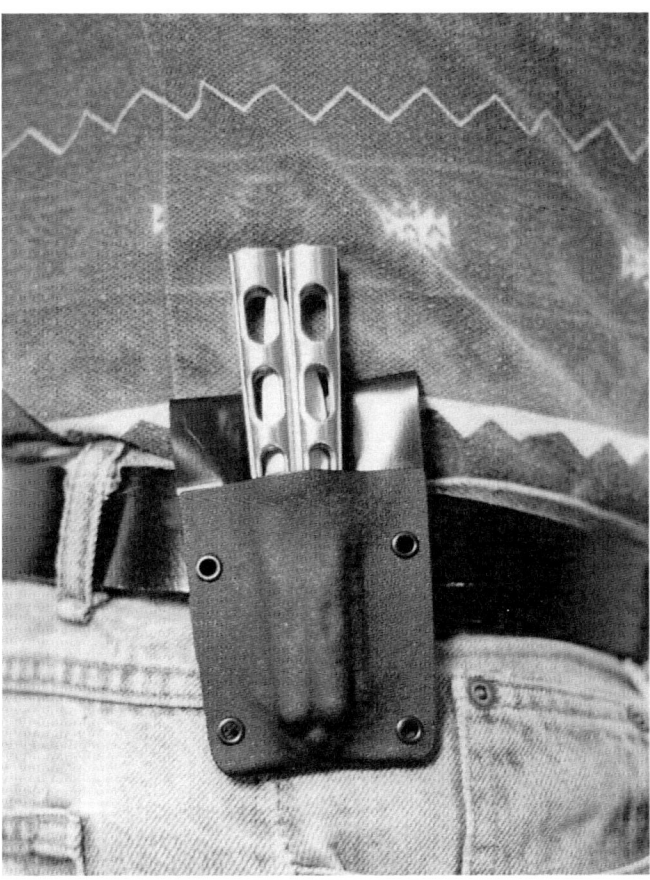

This is a custom belt scabbard designed by the author for a Benchmade latchless balisong. It was built to specs by the craftsmen of Cutlery Shoppe's Sheath-Tech division. The molded Kydex retains the knife securely without the need for snaps or straps, and the use of grommets allows the knife to be worn inverted as a neck carry rig. If your favorite knife happened to have come housed in a substandard sheath, give Cutlery Shoppe a call and have a Kydex rig made for it. Their work is top notch, and their prices are very affordable.

Knife pouches of this material not only don't last very long, they are also generally poorly designed. If you prefer a belt pouch carry and are looking for a good aftermarket pouch, both Cutlery Shoppe and Benchmade sell excellent pouches in a variety of sizes. Some folder fanciers have also adopted the police officer trick of carrying their knives in spare magazine pouches originally intended for autopistol magazines.

For the ultimate in a low-profile belt pouch, buy any one of the "multitool" gadgets that consist basically of folding pliers with an assortment of other tools built into the plier handles. Make sure that the tool comes in a sturdy belt pouch. Better yet, write the manufacturer and try to get a "new" pouch for your multitool (whether you actually have one or not). When you get the pouch, tuck your defensive folder into it and strap it to your belt. This is great camouflage for exotic folding fighters like balisongs since multitools have become so common that even people who typically get very upset at the sight of a knife in a belt pouch don't look twice when they see one. If someone asks to borrow your "tool," you can avoid the issue by claiming that whatever they need (screwdriver, bottle opener, etc.) is broken.

Of course, you can also have a belt pouch custom-made for your folder. Many leatherworkers offer knife pouches, and some will make special designs to their customers' specifications. Some knife designs also work well with molded Kydex pouches. The custom Kydex pouch that Cutlery Shoppe made for my latchless balisong not only works well when carried on a neck cord, it also features a Kydex belt loop. This design is particularly fast on the draw since its molded fit obviates the need for a retaining flap and allows more of the knife's handles to be exposed to be gripped by the drawing hand.

The second basic consideration in choosing a belt pouch is its *orientation*. By this I mean whether it secures to the belt with the mouth of the pouch facing upward, downward, or to the side. This is determined by the type of belt loop or loops attached to the back of the sheath.

The vertical upright carry is the most common belt pouch carry. The pouch is attached to the belt by means of a single belt loop that is attached lengthwise to its back panel. On better pouches, the bottom of this

Carrying a folder in a vertical upright pouch carry is secure and relatively benign looking; however, it does not provide for a quick draw.

as a vertical inverted carry. Drawing from this carry is faster and easier than from the upright carry since all the movements are directed downward. Releasing the pouch flap is accomplished with a downward brush of the thumb, leaving the four fingers curled beneath the mouth of the sheath to catch the knife, which typically slides right out of the pouch and into the hand. Again, the knife is repositioned in the hand for a one-handed opening.

The downside of this carry is that it appears much more aggressive and combat ready than an upright carry. The pouch is also susceptible to accidental openings, as the pouch flap has a habit of snagging on chair backs and seat belts as you stand up or exit a

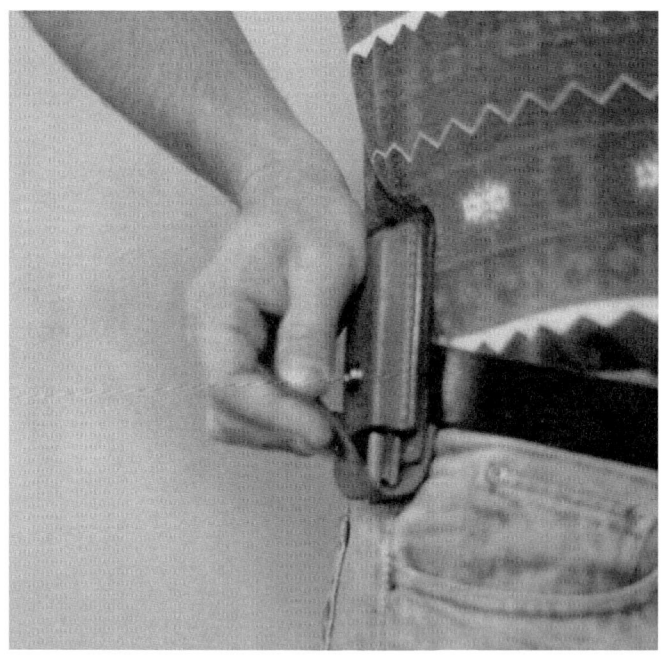

The vertical inverted carry offers a faster draw since the clearing line of the draw is more natural and gravity works in your favor. On the negative side, it presents a more aggressive appearance and is vulnerable to accidental flap release when you stand up from a seated position. This photo also demonstrates the proper method of releasing the flap prior to a draw. Note that the pouch is anchored to the hip by the heel of the hand and that the fingers do not leave contact with the pouch once the flap is released.

loop is secured via a snap fastener rather than permanent stitching. This makes it possible to attach and remove the sheath from the belt without having to remove the belt itself. To draw a knife from this carry, the retaining flap is released and the exposed portion of the closed knife is gripped with the index finger and thumb. The knife is then lifted vertically out of the pouch and regripped in the hand to allow for an appropriate one-handed opening.

The problem with the vertical upright carry is that lifting the knife vertically out of the pouch is difficult. The fingers are able to grip only a small portion of the knife handle, and the knife arm is forced into an uncomfortable position.

Belt pouches that are designed for vertical upright carries can also be worn upside down

Horizontal pouch carries are lower profile than vertical carries because the pouch blends with the line of the belt. The clearing line of the draw is very natural with the strong hand, but weak-hand draws are very slow and difficult. Here the author demonstrates a draw with a Benchmade custom balisong. Note that the locking latch is released automatically as the butt end of the knife clears the mouth of the pouch.

vehicle. You can avoid this by conditioning yourself to cover the pouch with your hand as you move.

Knife pouches can also be mounted on the belt horizontally. Pouches of this type have belt loops, or, in some designs, elastic belt "channels" attached perpendicularly to the length of the pouch. Horizontal pouches can be more comfortable to wear than pouches that ride vertically since they don't poke you when you sit down and don't snag on things when you get up. They also allow for faster draws than vertical upright pouches because the "drawing line" or path of your hand during the draw stroke is much more natural. Additionally, since horizontal pouches follow the line of the belt rather than running perpendicular to it, they can almost go unnoticed. Since a horizontal pouch doesn't extend below the belt line, it can be concealed effectively (if desired) under a short jacket. Choosing a pouch that closely matches the color of your belt can make this carry almost invisible.

There are two drawbacks to the horizontal pouch carry. Since the knife is mounted longitudinally to the belt and the belt follows the contour of the body, this carry only works well with shorter knives. Long knives tend to make the pouch stick out from the body, causing it to snag and making its presence painfully obvious. Additionally, unless the pouch is positioned directly on the side of the hip, it doesn't allow access to the knife with both hands.

Placement of the knife pouch on the belt is another important consideration in selecting a carry style. The guidelines for placement are virtually identical to those outlined in the section of this book devoted to waistband carries of straight blade knives. The only difference when dealing with belt pouches is that it is even more difficult to draw a folder from a pouch than it is to draw a fixed blade from a belt sheath. As such, you must experiment and try different positions to find what works best for you.

In general, the spot directly to the side of the hip on the strong side is the most versatile position with all pouch variations. It allows easy access with the strong hand and good access with the weak hand by reaching across the body. In a threatening situation, you can also assume a natural "hands on hips" position that allows you to discreetly lay your hand on your knife and either prime it for a quick draw or actually get it into your hand before trouble strikes.

In a vehicle, this carry position works well with the horizontal and vertical upright carries but requires that the pouch be twisted forward to draw from a vertical inverted carry.

Depending upon the style or styles of pants you wear, the positioning of your belt loops may vary considerably. To ensure that your knife pouch remains in the same place no matter what you wear, you should check the placement of the belt loops on all your pants. Any loops that are in the way of your preferred carry should be moved. It is also possible to either reposition or add belt loops as "stops" to keep the pouch from sliding on the belt during a draw. This is most helpful with horizontal carries since the force of withdrawing the knife runs in line with the length of the belt, making slipping a distinct possibility. Fortunately, tailoring belt loops is easy and reasonably cheap.

Like belt-mounted sheaths for fixed blades, pouches for folders should fit tightly on the belt without any slack or movement. A sturdy gun belt or other thick belt that is as wide as the attachment loop of the pouch will anchor the pouch securely and make for a fast, sure draw.

As with pocket carries, the placement of your knife in a belt pouch is critical to your ability to orient it in your hand automatically and open it immediately upon withdrawal. Since you will at best have only a partial grip on the handle of the knife when you remove it from the pouch, the knife must be placed so as to fall into the proper opening position *automatically* as soon as you complete your grip. Fumbling can mean lost seconds—and lost blood. *Your* blood.

For example, when you draw a knife from a vertical upright carry anywhere on the strong side of your body, you will initially be gripping only the last inch of the knife handle between the thumb and index finger of your strong hand. To assume a standard grip and to execute a standard grip opening, your thumb and index finger must grip around the pivot pin end of the handle and the closed blade must face away from your palm. Therefore, the best position for the knife in the pouch is with the pivot pin end up and the back of the closed blade facing forward. As the knife clears the pouch, the remaining fingers of the hand naturally curl around the handle as the thumb moves to open the blade. No repositioning or shifting of the knife is necessary.

To do this same type of opening from other pouch orientations, the placement of the knife within the pouch would be identical, only the orientation of the pouch would be different. A horizontal pouch is essentially a vertical upright pouch rotated 90 degrees downward. The knife would therefore be inserted in the pouch butt first with the back of the closed blade facing down. For an inverted vertical carry, it would be as if the vertical upright carry was rotated 180 degrees downward. The knife is placed in the pouch in exactly the same way, but the difference in the orientation of the pouch means the knife is carried butt end up with the back of the closed blade facing to the rear.

Note that in all the openings described here it is assumed that the belt pouch is worn somewhere on the strong side of the body. This can be anywhere from immediately to the side of the belt buckle to almost the center of the back, but nevertheless, on the side of the strong hand. The reason for this is that in most cases, this is the most accessible and therefore the most practical place to carry your knife. If, however, you prefer to carry your belt pouch in a crossdraw position, you can easily translate these instructions to your mode of carry by first placing the knife within the pouch in the manner described, then moving the pouch to the other side of your belt. As long as you still plan to acquire the knife with your strong hand, the drawing actions remain basically the same.

If you carry a standard folder and prefer a

reverse-grip opening, again you want to establish an initial grip on the knife as you draw that will remain unchanged once it is completely withdrawn from the pouch. To do this with a vertical upright carry on the strong side, you'll need to place your knife in the pouch so the butt end of the handle is upward and the back of the closed blade is facing forward. Your initial grip will again be with your thumb and index finger, this time gripping the butt end of the knife. As the knife clears the pouch, the other fingers close naturally around the handle and automatically into position for a ring finger or reverse-grip inertia opening.

As before, the placement of your knife in the pouch does not change for horizontal or inverted vertical carries. With these carries, it is as if the vertical upright carry is rotated 90 degrees and 180 degrees downward, respectively. If you have trouble visualizing this, take the pouch off your belt and hold it in the upright vertical carry position, then insert the knife as described above. Now put the pouch back on your belt in the desired carry position and remove the knife, making a careful mental note of how the knife was positioned so you can replace it the same way.

As I mentioned earlier, there are tricks to speed up draws from belt pouches. For leather pouches with snap fasteners, the tension of the snap is a major factor in determining the speed of your draw. Brand new pouches tend to have very stiff snaps that require considerable force to open and close. To loosen up the fit of these snaps, get a stout pair of needle nose pliers (preferably the kind with the flat tip) and insert the tips of the plier jaws into the female portion of the snap. Now, use both hands to spread the plier handles apart firmly but gently. Do this several times while rotating the pliers around the inner circumference of the snap fitting. This will spread the fitting slightly and make it easier to release.

You can also speed up your draw from a leather pouch by *carefully* trimming the

One way of speeding up a draw from a ballistic nylon pouch is to stiffen the pouch flap by inserting a finishing nail into the flap trim. The stiffened flap allows for a more solid grip and a more certain release.

pouch flap to make it narrower and trimming the sides of the pouch body just below the lip. The removal of leather in these strategic areas allows your fingers to get a better grip on the knife before you draw, making the draw more positive and consequently faster.

The technique you use to release the flap of your pouch also affects your drawing speed. If you pull the flap with your fingers, when the snap releases your fingers will actually leave contact with the knife and pouch. To complete the draw, you'll have to bring your hand back down to the pouch and reestablish a grip before you draw. Though the distances involved here are small, the fact that you lose contact with the pouch means that you have to reorient your hand before you draw, wasting precious time.

A better method is to place your fingers over the body of the pouch and anchor it to your side while popping the snap with your thumb. From this position you slide your hand up slightly to establish a grip with your thumb and index finger. The knife is then lifted out and the draw completed.

The problem with the flaps on most nylon knife pouches is that they are too flexible. Opening these pouches usually requires that you pinch the flap between your thumb and index finger and tear the Velcro loose. Needless to say, such precise movements are not easily accomplished when it's dark, time is of the essence, and your sphincter is severely puckered.

Fortunately, a simple modification that costs about a penny can solve this problem. Get a four-penny finishing nail and insert it into the trim around the bottom edge of the pouch flap. On some smaller pouches, you may have to trim the nail to get it to fit completely within the trim. This stiffens the edge of the pouch flap and makes it possible to open the pouch quickly by sliding your thumb and index finger under each side of the flap. By pressing your fingers against the body of the pouch rather than trying to pull the flap out away from the body, the pouch is anchored and stabilized. The release of the pouch flap leaves the thumb and forefinger positioned on each side of the exposed portion of the knife. This, of course, is the perfect position to grasp the knife and continue the movement into a smooth draw.

POUCH CARRIES FOR NONSTANDARD FOLDER DESIGNS

Belt pouches are also ideal homes for nonstandard folding knives such as the Barry Wood design, Paul knives, and balisongs. You must remember, however, that the pouch design and positioning must allow the knife to be acquired in a grip that allows it to be opened immediately without any prerequisite shifting in the hand.

The opening procedure for the Barry Wood design requires that it be held in a standard grip with the back of the closed blade facing your thumb. To acquire such a grip drawing from a belt pouch worn in a vertical upright carry, the knife must be placed in the pouch with the pivot pin up and the back of the closed blade facing rearward (assuming the knife is worn on the strong side). After the pouch flap is released in the approved manner, the thumb and index finger grasp the exposed portion of the handle and pull the knife straight upward. As it clears the pouch, the remaining fingers curl around the handle and the thumb slides down the back of the blade to begin the opening process.

As before, the placement of the knife within the pouch remains the same whether the pouch is worn horizontally or inverted.

Opening a Paul knife one-handed requires that it be grasped with the locking button pinched between the thumb and forefinger with the back of the blade facing you and the butt end of the handle pointing upward. To establish this grip from a vertical upright pouch draw (strong-side carry), you must place the knife in the pouch with the back of the closed blade facing forward and the handle butt down. The locking button is grasped between the thumb and forefinger while the knife is still in the pouch, and the knife hand should be bent sharply downward at the wrist. When the knife clears the pouch and the wrist is straightened, the knife will be positioned butt up and ready for the opening.

This technique works the same way for a horizontal carry, but unlike most horizontal carries in which the pouch mouth faces forward, this one works best with the pouch mouth facing to the rear. Once you establish a grip on the locking button, draw the knife straight back until it clears the pouch, then raise your hand up. You'll find it will be in a perfect position for a quick opening. The only disadvantage of this carry is that you can't anchor the pouch to your side with your fingers as you pop the pouch flap. To keep the pouch in place, find (or have made) pants that have a belt loop immediately to the rear of the spot where you prefer to place your pouch. This will prevent the pouch from sliding on the belt during the draw.

The strong-side vertical inverted carry with a Paul knife works best with the knife oriented so that the locking pin is down and the back of the closed blade faces rearward. The pouch flap is released by pushing the tips of the extended fingers under it so that once the snap or Velcro is released, the fingers are cupped beneath the mouth of the pouch. As the knife slides downward, your thumb reaches between the knife and the pouch to assume its position on the back of the locking button. The forefinger moves to the other side of the button. Once the grip on the button is established, pull the knife straight downward while maintaining a butt-up position. Raise your hand a few inches, push the locking button, and swing the handle downward to complete the opening.

Balisongs work very well when deployed from belt pouches because the pouch holds the knife in a specific predraw position. This allows you to automatically orient your hand on the safe handle during the draw so you can proceed immediately with an opening without fear of cutting yourself. Belt pouches also retain the handles of the balisong in the closed position, allowing the carry of latchless balisongs, which can be opened somewhat faster than models with locking latches. Nylon balisong pouches offer the best of both worlds in that the tight mouth of the pouch can be used to pop the latch of a latched balisong during the drawing movement. It can thus be opened as fast as a latchless model but retain the capability of being locked in the open position.

Earlier I described only two one-handed balisong opening methods. Though I will only explain the specific placement and drawing of the balisong for these two opening methods here, the same placement will work for many other opening techniques. Again, to determine how the knife must be placed in the pouch for a particular opening style, hold the knife in the preferred preopening position and, without changing its orientation, place it directly in the pouch. When you draw it, make sure that it comes out of the pouch and into your hand so it is automatically in the preopening position.

As detailed earlier, the upward swing opening is done by releasing the locking latch, then grasping the knife in a standard grip with the safe handle (the handle into which the unsharpened edge of the blade folds) against your palm and your palm turned down. Release the free handle and swing it upward toward the back of your hand. As the free handle nears your knuckles, curl your fingers around the underside of the safe handle and point your thumb outward. When the free handle reaches the end of its upward arc and strikes the safe handle, close your hand and complete your grip.

If you have a nylon pouch, you can do this opening directly from the draw. For a vertical upright carry (strong side), place the knife in the pouch butt first with the safe handle toward the rear. If you have a knife with a locking latch, fasten the latch only partway before inserting it in the pouch. This will ensure that the latch is released as the knife is drawn.

To draw and open the knife, release the pouch flap as previously described and grip the exposed portion of the knife between your thumb and forefinger. Balisongs with integral guards on the blades are easier to grip because the guards offer a solid purchase for the fingers. As you pull the knife upward out of the pouch, turn it slightly in your hand so the safe handle lies firmly against your palm. As the knife clears the pouch, you should hear the locking latch pop. If the pouch does not release it completely, you can finish the job using your free hand or by raking the end of the latch against your pant leg or a handy belt loop. Now drop your hand slightly into a palm-down position and perform the opening technique. If necessary, turn the knife in your hand to position the blade edge in accordance with your preferred knife-fighting style.

This style of opening works even better with horizontal pouches and vertical inverted carries, since the draw stroke is more comfortable when directed forward or downward. As always, the placement of the knife in the pouch is the same as the vertical upright carry; it is simply rotated 90 or 180 degrees downward, as appropriate.

The carry style and knife placement described above work equally well with practically all standard grip openings possible with a balisong. This method of drawing places the safe handle naturally in the palm, the position from which virtually all standard grip openings begin.

Now let's review the reverse forward swing opening. Hold the balisong inverted (butt end up) with the safe handle in the crotch of your thumb and your thumb pressing the closed knife against your curled fingers. Pop the locking latch with your thumb and swing the free handle forward. As it continues its arc, curl your fingers around the slotted side of the safe handle and point your thumb out to clear a path for the handle. Continue the arc of the free handle upward until it meets the safe handle, then close your hand to complete the grip. If necessary, turn the knife to position the blade edge outward.

The beginning grip for this opening is easily assumed by drawing from a vertical upright carry. Place the knife in the pouch with the butt facing upward and the safe handle (and the end of the locking latch) facing to the rear. After releasing the pouch flap, grip the exposed portion of the knife with your thumb and index finger and lift the knife out of the pouch. As the knife clears the pouch, turn it in your hand so your bent thumb is directly below the end of the locking latch. Once the knife is clear and you have a solid grip, pop the latch with your thumb and execute the opening.

This draw also works well from both the horizontal and vertical inverted carries. Placement of the knife in the pouch is once again identical to the upright carry. Also, the placement of the knife described here works well with virtually all possible reverse-grip opening methods.

It should be noted that most leather balisong pouches only allow the knife to be inserted tang first (leaving the butt end of the handles exposed). Most leather pouches are also only equipped for vertical carries. As such, these pouches are best suited for reverse-grip openings. If you're looking for an aftermarket belt pouch for your butterfly knife, the best source is Benchmade Knife Company of Clackamas, Oregon. They produce excellent leather and nylon pouches in several sizes for their line of custom and commercial balisong knives. Their "Cocoons" (all butterflies come from cocoons, right?) were also the original horizontal pouches on the market. Their best ones have a single elastic "tunnel" sewn to the back of the pouch that holds it very securely to the belt. Some of their more recent designs, however, use two nylon loops, which offer a rather sloppy fit, even on wide belts. The fit of these pouches can be improved by folding and stitching the belt loops to shorten them to the proper size.

CLIP-ON KNIVES

The greatest improvement in folding knife carry in recent years has been the introduction of clothing clips that allow knives to be clipped directly to an article of clothing. This idea was the brainchild of the innovative folks at Spyderco and, along with the round thumbhole in the blades, is an identifying characteristic of their "Clipit" line.

Advertisements for clip-on knives

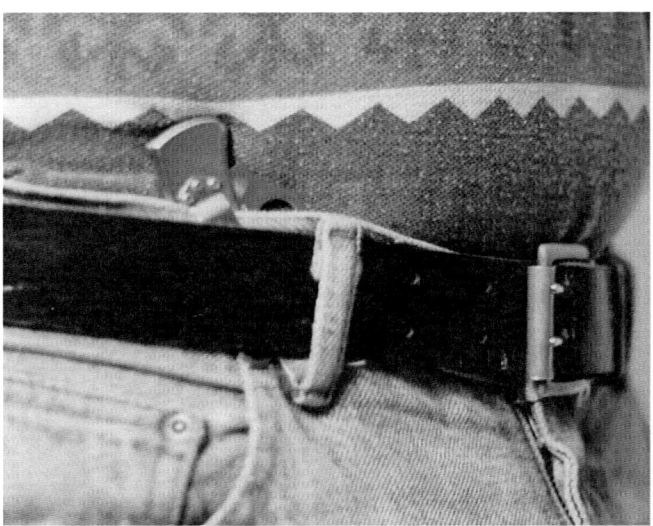

Clip-on knives, such as this Spyderco Police Model, are the most versatile carry knives available. The waistband carry, shown here, is compatible with anything from dress slacks to jeans to skirts to a pair of Speedos and is about as close as you can come to a universal carry method.

generally show the knife attached to the top of a side trouser pocket. While this is not a bad place to carry a knife, it does not do justice to the wide variety of carries that are possible with this design.

Remember that the idea in choosing a knife carry is to make it compatible with *all* the clothing in your wardrobe and *all* your styles of dress. Attached to the waistband, a medium-sized clip-on knife is compatible with everything from tuxedo trousers to a pair of Speedos. It is ideal for joggers and bikers (the bicycle kind) since it does not require a pocket or pouch to be carried. For women, it can be clipped on a skirt, pants, shorts, or even a bra. The latter carry is very discreet, yet instantly accessible, even while seated.

Clip-on knives offer several other important advantages over traditional folding knives. Most importantly, the clip allows them to be fastened to a variety of other things besides clothing. You can therefore tailor the placement of your knife to your environment to ensure that it remains instantly available. For example, if your normal carry is in your waistband on the strong side, you may find drawing the knife difficult when seated in a car. However, if you develop the habit of slipping the knife out of your waistband and clipping it to your seat belt when you get in the car, your knife remains literally at your fingertips. You could also clip it to the sun visor of your car, but I find that it is easier to forget it that way. The weight of your knife on the seat belt harness reminds you of its presence when you unfasten the belt, making it unlikely that you'll leave it behind.

Clip-on knives also leave no telltale signs of their presence, such as wear patterns in pockets or empty belt pouches. As such, they are easily ditched when the threat of a search looms.

Finally, many clip-on knives (at least most Spyderco models) are available in both left- and right-handed models. Both models can be opened with either hand, but the positioning of the clothing clip is reversed for the left-handed model, making it easier to wear and draw quickly on the left side of the body. This option makes it possible to carry two mirror-image knives and is probably the best solution to the problem of ambidextrous access. Even carrying two knives, the low profile of most clip-ons allows you to remain discreet. Wearing two belt pouches with a folder in each will certainly raise a few eyebrows.

The main consideration when choosing a clip-on knife is the placement of the clip. Some designs, such as Spyderco's metal handled knives, Benchmade's clip-on models, and the Gerber E-Z Out have pocket clips attached to the pivot pin end of the handle. When clipped to the pocket or waistband, they ride upright with the back of the closed blade facing forward. When drawn, the knife falls naturally into position for either a thumb opening or a blade grip/handle swing opening.

Some other clip-ons, such as Spyderco's

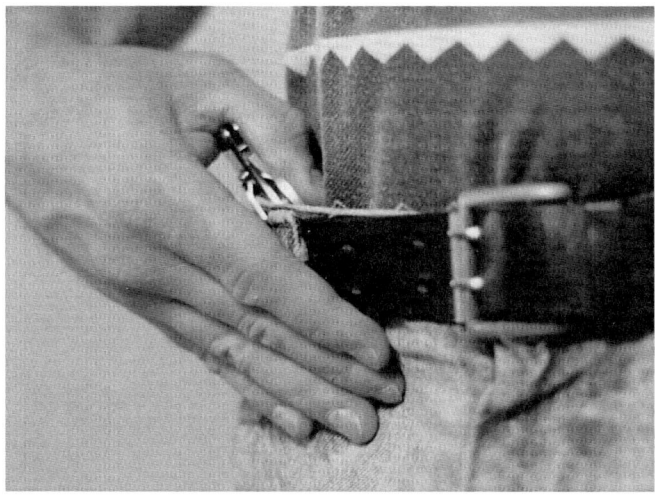

To draw a clip-on knife from a pocket or waistband carry, first press on the bottom end of the knife to create a gap between the upper end of the handle and your body. The thumb is then easily slid down to grip the knife. Jamming the thumb directly into the waistband is difficult and can result in a bruised thumb tip.

The positioning of a knife's clothing clip will determine whether it can be gripped during a draw and affects the ease with which certain one-handed opening methods can be performed. Spyderco's Endura Model has an integral plastic clip attached to the butt end of the handle, while its Wayne Goddard Custom Model features a stainless-steel clip attached to the pivot pin end of the handle.

Zytel-handled Clipits, Cold Steel Ultralocks, and the SOG Autoclip, have their clothing clips anchored to the butt end of the knife. The knife therefore rides inverted with the back of the closed blade facing to the rear. In this position, you must reach in deeper to grip the knife properly for a standard grip opening immediately from a draw.

If you are partial to reverse-grip openings, you'll find that you have to adjust the knife in your hand after you draw in order to position it properly. However, if you are a left-hander and get a right-handed model of a knife with a butt-mounted clothing clip, you're in luck. When worn on the left side, the knife rides inverted with the back of the closed blade forward. This is an ideal position for a draw and reverse-grip opening with the left hand. Naturally, if you are right-handed and can find a left-handed model of similar design, you can do the same thing.

To draw a clip-on knife with the clip attached to the pivot pin end of the handle from either a strong-side waistband or top-of-pocket carry, hook the top of the knife handle with your thumb and pull it away from your body. You can help this process by pushing on the bottom of the knife handle through your pants to create a see-saw effect. This preliminary move is important because it creates clearance for your thumb to slide down to grip the knife and indexes your hand on the knife prior to the draw. Slide your thumb about halfway down the length of the handle scale nearest your body and hook the tip of your index finger under the end of the clip on the outside of the pants. Now lift the knife upward. As it clears the top of the pocket or pants, slide it forward along the side of your body so the pressure on the butt of the knife causes it to

CARRY OPTIONS FOR FOLDING KNIVES

The waistband carry of a clip-on knife makes it very accessible, even in disadvantaged positions such as when caught by surprise from behind. Here a practiced draw and one-handed opening followed by some vigorous cutting on the choking arm quickly resolve the situation.

rotate in your hand into a standard grip. From here, you can proceed with either a thumb opening or standard grip inertia opening.

To do a blade grip/handle swing opening from this carry, after the initial move to create clearance for the thumb, slide the thumb down into position on the side of the blade and hook the index finger under the clip. As you lift the knife and it begins to clear the top of the pants or pocket, the index finger slides into position on the other side of the blade. When the knife is completely out, turn your elbow down and your hand up to invert the knife, then proceed with the opening.

For knives with clothing clips attached to the butt end of the handle, the drawing technique is pretty much the same except that the thumb must be thrust deeper inside the pants or pocket so it can grasp at least two-thirds of the handle before beginning the draw. This will prevent fumbling during the draw and position the hand well for any standard grip opening technique.

Knives of this type can be drawn and opened with a blade grip/handle swing opening, but it requires that the knife be spun 180 degrees in the hand after the draw to assume a proper grip. This works reasonably well with knives with blade opening holes but is at best a risky proposition in a self-defense situation.

In my opinion, clip-on knives are one of the best choices in personal defense blades. The fact that they can be worn in the same position with a wide variety of clothing styles makes them much less likely to be left at home than knives that require more complicated carries. The fact that they are popular with law enforcement officers and paramedics also makes them more socially acceptable than a substantial folder carried in a belt pouch. If you plan to buy only one personal defense knife for everyday carry, make it a clip-on folder.

IMMINENT DANGER AND COVERT DRAWS

By staying alert and aware of what's going on around you, you can avoid many confrontations before they occur. If you cannot avoid trouble, a properly chosen carry method, along with sufficient amounts of practice, will allow you to react to a threatening situation and have your knife in hand in less than two seconds. While this may seem fast, if you are truly surprised by an attack, it may not be fast enough.

Anytime you are going to be in a setting where you feel you may not be able to draw your knife quickly enough to respond to an attack, you should draw your knife first and enter with it in hand. Obviously, if anyone else is around, openly brandishing a blade will cause some alarm, so we need to examine methods of drawing a knife discreetly and carrying it secretly while in full view of others.

Ultimately, you want to develop the ability to draw your knife quietly and discreetly and move through an unsecure area with it undetected. When the threat has passed, you should be able to replace your knife in its carry position just as discreetly as you drew it. For example, when leaving a building to go to your car, you should have your car key ready to go in your weak hand and your knife in your strong hand before you step out the door. In the security of your locked car, you can put your knife back in its carry position (if it is practical for a seated draw) or keep it at hand next to you. Before you leave your car to enter your house, your house keys should be in your weak hand ready to go and your knife in your strong hand before you open the car door.

In case you're wondering, if you're carrying a bag or package, the same procedure applies. Your keys and knife go in your hands first, then you pick up anything else you need to carry. If an object can be carried with one hand, make it your weak hand so you can keep your knife hand free and ready to move.

In the section on object carries, we discussed several techniques of carrying a knife ready for instant use while in full view of others. For example, a knife can be held in the hand and covered by a paper bag or envelope. If you have the time to set them up, such carries are great for going into threatening situations. In fact, it's not a bad idea to carry a second knife rigged in this manner in addition to your normal carry blade.

If you find yourself stuck in a threatening situation and all you have is your normal carry blade, a *covert draw* and *imminent danger carry* will allow you to put that knife quietly in your hand ready for instant use.

Covert draws are not much different from regular drawing methods. The movements are usually identical; however, they are performed more slowly and under the disguise of other

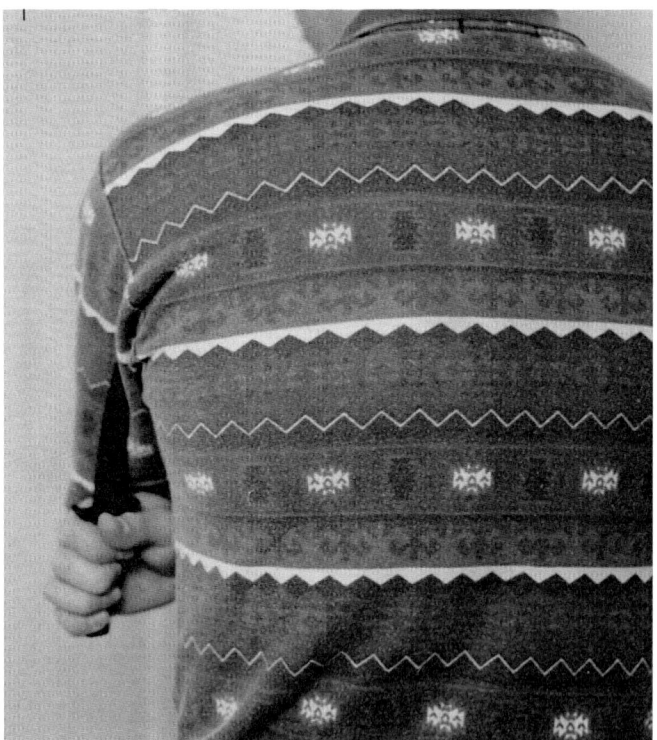

If you sense that you might need to use your knife and can't exit the area, the safest bet is to have your knife in hand and be ready. Here a fixed blade knife is concealed behind the upper arm by assuming an arms-folded posture. The knife is a vintage Gerber Mark I that has had its blade blued. Subdued blade finishes of this type are actually more practical for concealing imminent danger carries on the street than for stalking and silencing sentries.

natural actions. For example, I described earlier how a benign movement like folding your arms can set you up for a draw from a shoulder harness. If you want to go a step further but stop short of actually brandishing your blade, cross your arms as described earlier and draw your blade from its sheath. Then, under the cover of your weak-side upper arm, move the knife outside your jacket and conceal it behind that arm. From this position, you are poised for instant cutting and thrusting.

If you carry a fixed blade knife or folder in any other carry position, you can also draw it discreetly and move to this position when things get tense. The key to any covert draw is to try to cover or disguise the movement with another action. Drawing a knife from a strong-side inside-the-pants carry may seem tremendously high profile, but if you camouflage the movement by putting your hands on your hips or scratching your ribs, it is much less obvious. The key to making covert draws really covert is practicing them in conjunction with natural movements. A bad covert draw can be more obvious than simply making a direct move for your blade. Practice and feeling at ease carrying a weapon will allow you to get it out without attracting attention.

On a related subject, making sure that your knife is where it's supposed to be without drawing attention to it is also a critical skill. Discreet *weapon checks* can be done by naturally scratching yourself, hiking up your pants, tucking in your shirttail, or reaching for your comb or wallet. Depending upon your preferred carry and the movement you choose, it may be more natural to touch your knife with your wrist or forearm than your hand.

The most popular method of secretly carrying a knife in the hand is to grip it in a reverse grip and tuck the blade behind your wrist. This works best if you're wearing a jacket or long-sleeve shirt, since the sleeve material can help draw attention away from the blade. It is just as effective, however, if your arms are bare. This is not a full, tight reverse grip, but rather a half grip with the thumb that allows the fingers to remain extended and appear natural. From this carry position, you can execute a surprise forehand slash followed by a backhand stab to an opponent in front of you. Backhand stabs from this position to the groin, thighs, or abdomen will discourage any surprise attacks from the rear.

A variation of this carry that completely conceals the knife from view is to draw it with a reverse grip and fold your hands in front of you. Place your knife hand closest to your body so the knife blade is concealed between your body and your wrist, then fold

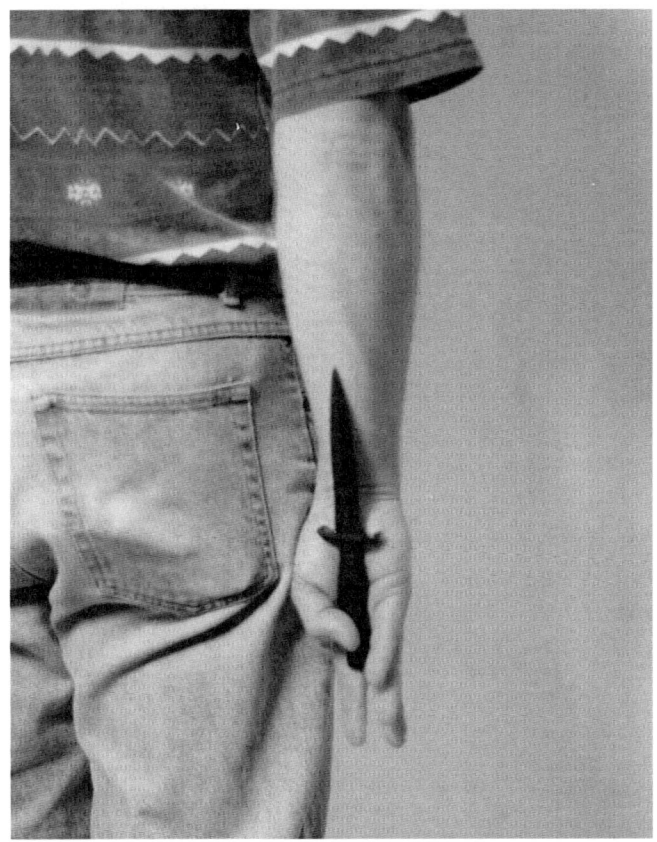

The classic imminent danger posture with a knife is to simply hold it in a reverse grip with the blade concealed behind your wrist. A loose grip, as shown here, allows the hand to appear more natural and is less likely to be spotted.

When trouble looms, having your weapon in hand is your best bet. Faced with the threat of a knife-wielding attacker, our hero has prepared himself by concealing his own knife behind his wrist. The attacker's thrust is deflected by a lead-hand parry and countered with an ice pick stab to the knife arm. This disables that limb and causes the attacker's head to lurch forward. Grabbing the attacker's hair for control, the defender exposes his neck and finishes the fight with a powerful downward stab to the subclavian artery.

If you wear a jacket with rear-facing pockets, an excellent imminent danger carry is to grasp your knife in a reverse grip and stick your hand loosely into your pocket. This works particularly well against attacks from behind, as the knife can be withdrawn and thrust backward in one fluid motion, as shown here.

your other hand over the top.

My favorite version of this carry is to use it with a jacket with pockets that open to the rear. A fixed blade or opened folding knife can be held in a reverse grip and the hand placed *mostly* within the pocket to completely conceal the knife from view. Do not put the hand all the way in the pocket, or it may snag when you try to remove it in a hurry. This carry allows you to keep your hands warm without gloves during cold weather and offers an instant response to a hostile threat.

In recent years, both custom and commercial knife makers have been offering an increasing number of knives with "subdued" blades. Bluing, phosphate coating, Teflon coating, and bead blasting have all been used to make knife blades nonreflective, ostensibly for military use where light discipline is required. In reality, these blades (at least the smaller ones) are better suited for imminent danger street carries where reflection and light discipline are *really* a problem. If you plan to use imminent danger carries frequently, look for a knife with a subdued finish or have your present carry knife bead blasted to dull its finish.

As explained earlier, your ultimate goal in imminent danger carries is to be able to draw *and* replace your knife without anyone being the wiser. With some carries, like shoulder harness, inside-the-pants, and neck cord carries, this can be difficult. Rushing to the bathroom every time you enter a building so you can stow your knife is a habit that could raise some suspicions. Carrying a small folding knife in addition to your main defensive blade is one way of dealing with an imminent threat. This knife can be used for an initial defensive response to buy time to draw your main blade. Ultimately, however, tailoring your tactics and carry to *your* needs is the only way to come to a happy compromise between discretion and preparedness.

An alternative to carrying a naked blade and having to resheath it every time you enter a safe area is to select a carry system that allows you to remove the knife *and* the sheath easily. Even if you're spotted with your knife, the fact that it's in a sheath will make it much less threatening than an exposed blade. Unsheathing your knife can be accomplished very quickly by grasping the sheath with your free hand or your teeth and releasing the blade.

For this type of carry, my favorite knives are Cutlery Shoppe's Gryphon M10 boot knife with an inside-the-pants Kydex sheath and any of Bud Nealy's knives in an MCS sheath. The belt loop on the Gryphon's Kydex sheath has a snap that allows you to remove it and replace it easily. Nealy's MCS sheath in either the inverted center-of-back carry or inside-breast-pocket carry can simply be slid out and clutched in the hand. Both of these sheaths feature simple but effective knife retention systems that free their blades easily should the need arise.

Imminent danger carries with folding knives are easier than with fixed blades because they can be done with the knife blade closed. Many folders can be completely concealed in the hand, making it very difficult for casual observers to realize that you are armed. Covert draws of folding knives are basically the same as full-speed draws but have the added advantage that it is much harder to identify a closed folding knife than it is a straight knife with a gleaming blade. Once you have a folder in your hand, you can react to a threat and open your knife in less than a second if you've mastered a good one-handed opening technique. Better yet, you can anticipate the threat and open your knife in advance.

As with a fixed blade knife, when carrying a folder in the hand you should not grip it too tightly. Not only does this betray its presence, it can also cause your hand to sweat or cramp after a while. When you use your thumb to hold it to your palm and leave your fingers extended, your hand appears much more natural and the carry is more comfortable.

Instead of carrying a folder in your hand, you might choose to wear it on a lanyard around your wrist. Most quality folding knives come with lanyard holes in the handle. If your knife doesn't have one, find a friend with a drill press and a little machining knowledge and you should be able to drill a neat hole that will not adversely affect your knife's form and function. Then just thread a length of parachute cord or similar material through the hole and tie it off so that it just fits over your hand. You can go a step further if you want and slip a large wooden or plastic bead over both of the free ends of the cord before you tie them off. This way you can tie the loop so it slides over your hand easily and slide the bead up or down to adjust the fit on your wrist. When this is done properly, the wrist thong will let the knife dangle high enough so it remains hidden behind the fingers but low enough so it doesn't restrict your opening technique.

The advantage of the wrist thong carry is that it makes it impossible for you to drop your knife in a fight. However, it also

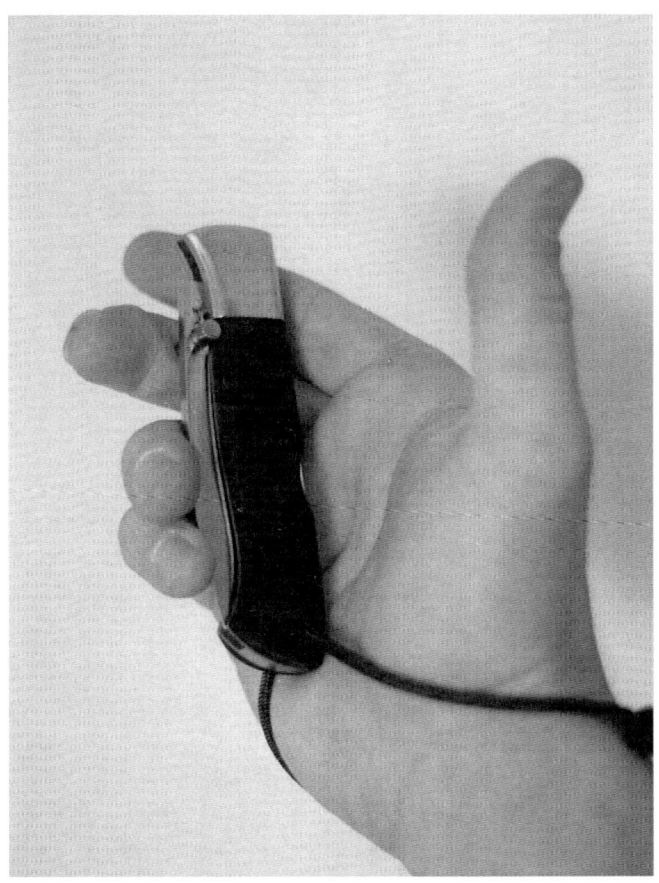 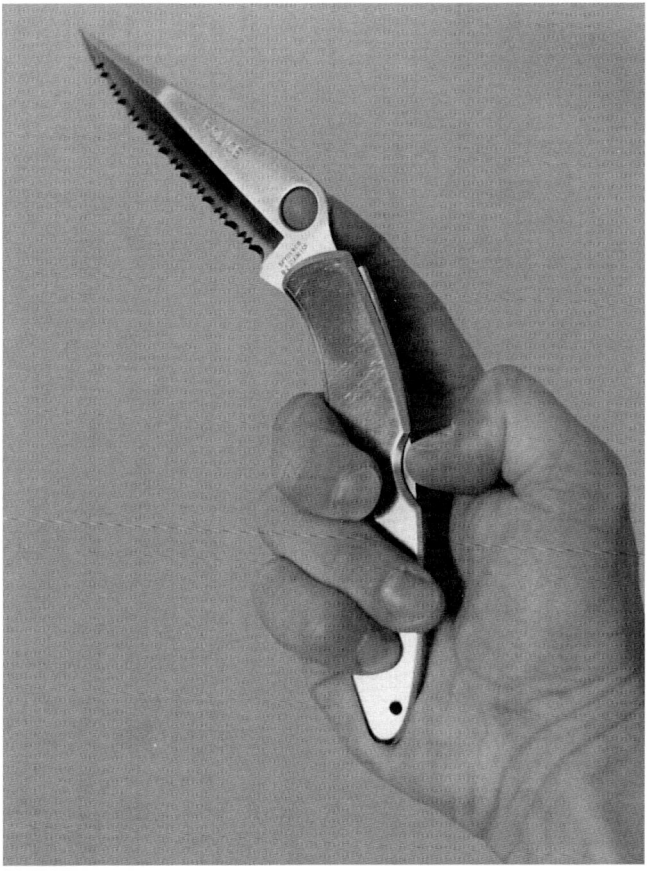

One sneaky way of keeping a lockblade folding knife available is to wear it on a wrist lanyard. Adjust the length of the lanyard so the knife hangs in a comfortable position for an immediate one-handed opening, yet remains concealed by the relaxed hand and fingers.

If you carry a folder, in addition to being able to carry it covertly, you should have the ability to open it covertly with one hand. Covert openings begin with standard one-handed opening methods that stop short to avoid the telltale snap of a blade locking into place. The remainder of the opening is completed slowly and noiselessly by applying pressure to the locking bar as the blade is opened. Here a standard thumb opening is completed silently by working the locking bar with the thumb while the index finger moves the blade into the locked position.

prevents you from switching to a reverse grip or passing the knife to your weak hand. As with any other carry decision, take these facts into account and factor them into your own personal equation to determine what works for you.

Similar to covert draws are covert openings with folding knives. These openings are essentially silent versions of the one-handed openings that have already been described. The only difference is that you don't open the blade completely with the initial movement so you can avoid the unmistakable "snap" of the blade locking in place. Instead, you open the blade about three-quarters of the way with the normal technique, then slowly ease it the rest of the way under firm control. For lockback knives, it's even better if you can operate the locking mechanism during the final stage of the opening to totally eliminate the sound of the

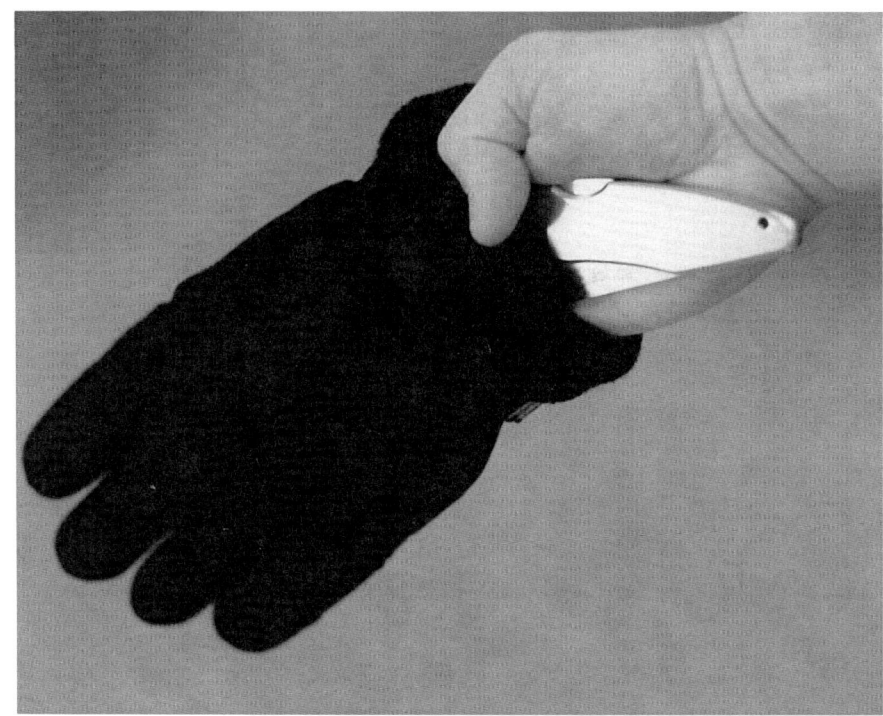

Drawing a knife from concealment while wearing winter gloves is slow and difficult. A better solution is to load a closed folding knife into your glove before you go out in the cold. In this position, the knife can also be used as a palm sap to deliver a stunning slap before removing the glove and bringing the blade into action.

blade snapping into place.

For example, a silent version of the thumb opening with a lockback knife would begin as usual but stop with the blade short of fully opened. The thumb would then depress the lock release, and the index finger would move the blade into the fully opened position. Once the blade is fully opened, the locking bar is released to silently lock the blade in place.

This method works well with center lock knives such as Spyderco lockbacks. For knives with full-length locking bars such as Buck folders, it is impossible to work the lock release and open the blade with your index finger at the same time. With these knives, open the blade by pressing the point or side (not the edge) against your pant leg while you operate the lock release. The result is still a silent opening that, when done discreetly, puts an open knife in your hand without the other guy knowing it's there.

Most one-handed openings, with the obvious exception of inertia openings, can be adapted to silent openings. Do the opening, but stop short. Then experiment and find the easiest and most comfortable way to get the blade open the rest of the way without making any noise.

Although opening a balisong quietly may seem impossible (after all, one of its nicknames is the "click-clack"), it isn't. The trick is pointing the knife downward so gravity accomplishes what inertia and momentum do in full-speed openings.

One of the biggest problems with carrying a folder or any other knife for personal defense comes when cold weather hits. In cold weather, wearing gloves is common practice. Gloves, however, can make drawing a knife quickly almost impossible. Usually, they do not provide enough grip or "feel" to draw a fixed knife effectively, let alone draw *and open* a folder. Going without gloves can leave your hands numb and stiff, a condition which, sadly, does not promote deft knife handling either.

My answer to this problem is to wear your gloves and stick your folder right inside them. No matter where you normally carry your folder, when you bundle up to step out in the cold, draw your closed knife and slip it down inside your strong-hand glove. In most cases, it will lie comfortably across your palm and still allow you reasonable dexterity with your fingers. If you need to use the knife, simply withdraw your thumb from its position in the glove and use it to hold the knife to your palm. Then, with your free hand or your teeth, pull the glove off your hand, open the knife, and commence cutting. If you pull your glove off with your free hand, don't forget to toss it in your attacker's face to get his guard up while you unzip his stomach with your knife.

An additional benefit of this particular carry is that the closed knife hidden in your glove can also be used to deliver a nasty blow to open the fight. For example, caught unaware and unable to draw your blade (God forbid), you might, in what is a natural response, raise your hands and tell your attacker you don't want any trouble. From this position, a sudden open-hand slap with your concealed knife will stagger him and give you time to open your blade.

For you historians, this application of the knife is similar to a somewhat obscure item called a *palm sap*. This is a lead-filled leather bubble attached to a small band, much like a watchband. The band fits around the back of the hand so the lead-filled sap rests in the palm. Palm saps were popular among policemen in the early part of the 20th century since they were practically invisible, yet extremely effective. Just think of the respect a beat cop would earn when the whole neighborhood saw him knock some troublemaker senseless with a single open-handed slap.

Another method of using gloves in imminent danger carries involves hunting mittens with a flap in the palm to allow the index finger to poke out and squeeze a trigger. Inserting the blade of a push dirk through this flap, then donning the mitten, creates a very nasty improvised gauntlet. The flap actually retains the knife, allowing the fingers to relax. When needed, the fingers retract and curl around the knife handle before a blow is struck. The problem with this carry is that the finger portion of the mitten can get in the way of the blade. When thrusting this won't matter much, though, and that's about all you'll be doing with a push dirk anyway.

While we're on the subject of gloves, I should add that a good pair of gloves can be a great asset in a knife fight, providing protection to both your knife hand and free hand. Thanks to the AIDS scare, a whole industry has developed to produce cut- and puncture-resistant gloves for police officers to conduct personal searches without fear of

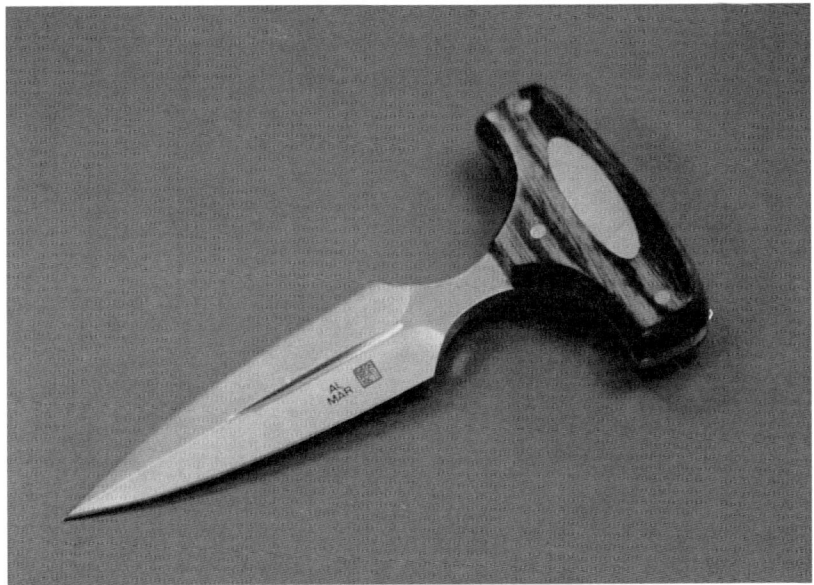

Another good carry method when forced to wear gloves is to conceal a push dirk such as this one by Al Mar Knives in a pair of hunting mittens with a trigger finger flap. The blade is pushed through the flap and the handle is retained within the mitten. When a situation arises, the fingers retract to close around the handle to deliver a quick punch-style thrust.

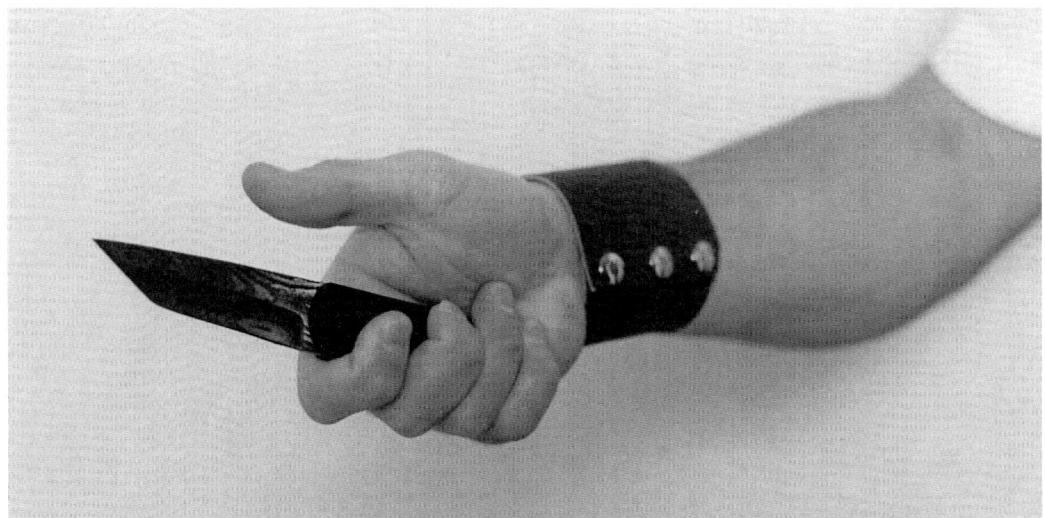

Any protection you can wear will give you an advantage in a knife fight. Here a wrist gauntlet is used to protect the vulnerable inner wrist area. Leather jackets, cut-resistant gloves, and even body armor are also worthwhile investments.

being jabbed by a junkie's needle. These gloves are typically lined with Kevlar, the same material used in body armor, but are thin enough to provide adequate tactile feel for an effective search. Needless to say, a cut-proof glove is a definite advantage to a knife fighter. And, although this discussion of gloved carries has been concerned mostly with cold weather conditions, there are no rules preventing the wearing of gloves in warm weather.

On a similar note, any type of clothing or accessory that can protect you from an opponent's cut or thrust is a worthwhile investment. If your style of dress allows, leather wrist gauntlets can provide protection for the vulnerable blood vessels and tendons of the wrist. If this is too obvious, a wide, heavy leather watchband is a good second choice.

In a more general sense, a leather coat is much harder to cut through and absorbs the shock of a blow more readily than a thin jacket. Jeans are more resilient than dress slacks. Long-sleeve shirts afford greater protection than short-sleeve ones. You get the idea.

If you're really concerned and can afford it, soft body armor is a worthwhile addition to your wardrobe. Competition in this field and advances in fabric technology have driven prices down, making vests accessible to even those with limited personal defense budgets. When shopping for soft armor, make sure you check its resistance against knife attacks as well as bullets, since many ballistic vests that stop bullets effectively can still be punctured by a strong knife thrust.

Conclusion

The decision to carry a personal defense knife is not a simple one. If you think tucking a knife in your pocket or strapping one on your belt is enough to make you safe from street crime, you're sadly mistaken. People who are serious about carrying personal defense knives are necessarily serious about using them. They seek out instruction in knife fighting, select their blades and carry systems carefully, and practice their skills regularly. Perhaps more than any other type of martial artist, they strive to cultivate a warrior mentality.

This type of intense commitment and a determination to survive are the primary attributes needed to use a knife effectively in self-defense. Just carrying a knife doesn't mean that you have what it takes to draw it under stress and purposefully cut or stab another human being with it. When you combine commitment, determination, solid knife-fighting skills, a knife and carry system suited to your needs, and a good dose of common sense, the result is a very prepared, very dangerous individual. This is your goal. I hope the information in this book helps you achieve it.

Sources

Al Mar Knives, Inc., 5755 SW Jean Rd., Ste. 101, Lake Oswego, OR 97035. The late Al Mar was one of the most talented knife designers ever and one of the first to devote consistent efforts to commercially produced defensive bladeware. His designs live on in the current AMK line, which includes many models that are well-suited for defensive use.

Benchmade Knives, Inc., 15875-G SE 114th St., Clackamas, OR 97015. Producers of an assortment of personal defense knives, as well as the finest custom and production balisongs available today.

Cold Steel, Inc., 2128 Knoll Drive, Unit D, Ventura, CA 93003. Producers and retailers of a wide variety of knives, including many designs suitable for personal defense use.

Cutlery Shoppe, 5461 Kendall St., Boise, ID 83706-1248. The premier mail order cutlery retailer in the U.S., Cutlery Shoppe offers a tremendous selection of production knives at prices well below most stores. It also boasts a "Sheath-Tech" division that produces high-quality custom Kydex sheaths for both production and hand-crafted blades.

Gerber Legendary Blades, 14200 SW 72nd Ave., Portland, OR 97281. One of the largest cutlery manufacturers in the U.S. and one of the first commercial companies to offer knives designed for personal defense.

Bud Nealy, 822 Thomas St., Stroudsburg, PA 18360. Designer and maker of the excellent Multiple Concealment Sheath (MCS) system, a Kydex sheath system that includes matching mounting hardware for a wide variety of carry styles. This unique system allows the buyer to experiment with different carry methods and is the only complete carry *system* I've seen offered. In addition to its different carry options, Nealy's MCS features a brilliant magnetic retention feature that holds the knife securely even when inverted yet allows for a lightning-quick draw.

James S. Piorek ("Blade Rigger"), P.O. Box 5032, Missoula, MT 59806. One of the most innovative designers and makers of custom knife carry systems in business today. Piorek offers a tremendous variety of carry systems mated perfectly with a wide selection of custom knives, most of which feature Japanese design characteristics.